The Dual Family Guide to

Creating a Happy Family
Under Two Roofs After Divorce

Marguerite

Thank you for your
interest in this subject.
It's an important one.
All the best!

D Riley

The Dual Family Guide to

Creating a Happy Family
Under Two Roofs After Divorce

DD Richards

BEST LIFE BOOKS™

Morgan Hill, California
www.DualFamily.com

Editor and Project Manager: Marla Markman
www.MarlaMarkman.com
Cover and Book Design: CenterPointe Media
www.CenterPointeMedia.com

Library of Congress Control Number: 2012923426
ISBN: 978-0-9887076-0-3
Printed in the United States of America

Dedication

To my amazing son, who is the reason we work every day to be a happy dual family. You are my world. I love you deeply!

To Grant and Deb, who have embraced our family and nurtured it every step of the way. Thank you for being a great dad and a wonderful second mom to Evan. I appreciate you both so very much.

To Marc, who willingly jumped on our dual family bandwagon. You have been so supportive and encouraging of our family. You are a dream come true.

To all my wonderful friends and family who saw me through putting this book together. Thank you for your constant words of encouragement, for reading everything I asked, for helping me in any way you could, and most of all, for believing in me. You are treasures, and I love you.

A special thanks to singer, songwriter, and friend, Michael McNevin, for the use of the Mudpuddle shop, where much of this book was written.

To all those living with divorce, this book is for you. There is a light at the end of the tunnel, so keep moving forward. I wish you all the success and happiness possible in this world.

*"When writing the story of your life,
don't let anyone else hold the pen."*
—UNKNOWN

*"Thank you, Brian, for showing me how to hold my own pen.
I am eternally grateful."*

Contents

Preface

I do a lot of business travel, and a few years ago during my journeys, an interesting thing happened. When I met new people, we would make the obligatory introductions and, quite often, people would ask me more questions about myself: "Where are you from?" "Do you have children?" "What does your husband do?" My response was generally, "I'm from Silicon Valley. I have one amazing son who loves basketball, and I'm not married."

It was the last comment, "I'm not married," that, strangely enough, led to this book. When I told people that my husband and I were divorced, nine times out of ten they responded with something like "Oh, that's terrible. That must be so difficult on you and your son." My general reply was "No, actually, it's really good! We get along extremely well, we live just a couple of minutes from each other, and we still do lots of family things together. It's a great arrangement for us, and our son benefits from still having us be together, just not every day." I know my family situation is a little different from most because people usually looked at me a little cross-eyed and said something to the effect of "Wow, that's really unusual." Now here's the kicker. There was a two month or so period of time when I met loads of new people, and the comment I heard from most of them at the end of our introduction was "Your family situation is so unusual and sounds so healthy. You should write a book about it." After hearing that more than a dozen times from different people, I started to think about it.

I'm not a writer, therapist, marriage counselor, or child psychologist; I'm just a mom, a regular person who wanted the best life possible for her child. Knowing that I didn't have any important credentials or initials after my name, I was concerned about my ability to write a book and possibly give other people advice. So I sought out additional opinions and took an informal poll of divorced parents about the viability of a book like this. Would there be a market for it? Would people trust me with the information I'm giving them? Would divorced couples want to get along and become better families? The answers I received were a resounding "Yes!" So here I am.

We've been divorced for more than a decade now, and I thought I pretty much knew everything there was to know about our divorce and our current family relationship. I realize now that I didn't know as much as I thought. While writing, I was able to dig a little deeper and look back with fresher eyes and see things in a way I hadn't quite before. Through the process of writing the book, I learned a lot about my marriage and divorce, my ex-husband, and our family dynamic. But most important, I learned a ton about me.

Preface

Going through a divorce really isn't about the person you're divorcing. It's about you. If you realize that early on, you'll save yourself a lot of pain and agony trying to blame someone else when all you can do in any situation is focus on you and your actions. How you deal with issues in your divorce not only affects your ex, but it affects you and your children. I know that may seem obvious, but in the heat of the moment, we can easily lose sight of that, and that's when we're most likely to make mistakes.

This book was a deeply personal experience for me. In it, I share some of my most intimate and raw moments, where I was at my weakest—maybe at my worst—as well as my darkest fears, aha moments, and best practices so, hopefully, you won't have to go through years of learning these lessons the hard way like I did. While I would truly not prefer to show this side of myself to the world, I think it's important I pull the curtain back and let you know that I'm human, I make mistakes, so do you, and it's OK. The challenge is, how do you recover from those mistakes and build a better future for you and your family? It can be done. I did it and continue to do it every day with our family. It took me a while, but I figured it out, and with the desire to create a happy divorced family and the help of me and this book, I'm betting you can, too.

If you want to create a happier family and a happier you after divorce, to help your kids thrive in your divorced family, to start living the life of your dreams—and you want real-life examples to show you the way—this book is for you. Here you'll get practical insight to situations you may have experienced or are likely to experience in your divorced family and suggestions on how to overcome them and deal with them. You'll get real solutions to real problems and ideas on how to improve your family that you can implement immediately. Through the exercises in the book you'll discover more about yourself and be able to work through your challenges successfully on your own timeframe, in your own way. I have more than a decade of experience bringing my divorced family from "what a mess to a great success!" I'm proof that just about anyone can have a happy family life after divorce. Why not you?

You may think that life after divorce will never be full and wonderful and exciting again, but I promise you, there is a light at the end of the tunnel, so keep moving forward. And remember, you can achieve amazing things if you just keep trying. I wish you and your family all the success and happiness this world has to offer. Now go get it!

All my best and remember, think happy!

Introduction
A Better Approach to Divorce

"Never say that you can't do something,
or that something seems impossible, or that
something can't be done, no matter how
discouraging or harrowing it may be...."
—Mike Norton

Divorce is one of the most difficult life changes you'll have to deal with. It doesn't matter if you are the divorcer or the divorcee. A major break-up is full of intense emotions, regrets, what-if's, what-could-have-beens, and the anguish of second-guessing your decisions. All this is made worse when there are children involved. The guilt a parent feels when considering divorce can be unbearable. It certainly was for me. Not knowing the effect the divorce would have on my son throughout his formative childhood years was awful and filled me with guilt.

Divorce may not be easy, but I believe there are ways for couples to avoid the nastiness, backstabbing, and general bickering that inevitably occurs in the midst of most divorces, and learn to happily move into separate and new lives. You can even, dare I say, learn to live in a caring, friendly existence with your ex. You may not think this is a possibility, but the *Dual Family Guide* is here to help you do just that.

Although there is a huge emphasis on children in divorce, it isn't all about the kids. Our children are a large part of why we want and need to be at our best, to set the right example, and show them the right way to treat others so they grow up to be great people. But this is about your life, too. Over the years I've found that the more at peace I was with my ex and the smoother our relationship was, the happier I was. The positive relationship I created with my ex spilled over into the rest of my life, and I was happier in every aspect. Now, this didn't happen overnight, and it's something I have to work toward on a regular basis, but consider the alternative.

How does the average divorce normally look? You know the drill: There are usually attorneys involved; sometimes long, drawn-out court battles that cost a small fortune; huge fights over money and possessions; the children are often used by the parents to get back at each other; the kids suffer; the parents suffer; no one is truly happy. Sound familiar? What if it doesn't have to be like that? What if there was a different way to approach divorce and your family after divorce? What if you could still have family events with your children and your ex, and have fun and enjoy each other like a family but live under two separate roofs? What if there was a way to make over your divorced family into a happy, constructive and interactive *dual family*?

What in the world is a dual family? It's what my divorced family is, and it's wonderful! Instead of being one family under one unhappy roof, we are now two families in two very happy and separate homes. One family consists of my son, me and my partner, Marc, and the other family is made up of my son, my ex-husband, his wife and her two kids from a previous marriage. Our son is what connects us. Each family lives in their own home and we communicate regularly, almost on a daily basis. My son and I frequently do our own thing and live our lives within our family, but all seven of us also come together from time to time as a dual family. We share birthdays and some holidays together, and make decisions about vacations and schedules, doctor appointments, school issues, and other important things, just like a traditional family does. It's a wonderful way to exist after a divorce, and everyone is happy. I'm not saying it's a walk in the park, but the payoffs sure are great if you can make it work.

I was able to get to where I am now by focusing on what was really important, taking a lot of time to reflect on my marriage and my role in it, how I wanted my life to look and the kind of wonderful life I wanted my son to have and knew he deserved. As a result, our dual family is thriving. Everyone is content and happy and loving toward each other. In fact, we're much happier now than when we were married. Getting here wasn't easy. Sometimes it seemed for every step I took forward, I took three steps back, but I got here, and you can, too.

You can have a thriving family with your ex, your kids can grow up in a loving family that just happens to not live under one roof, and you can be deliriously happy with all of it. It's true! But you have to do the work. You have to focus on the big goals, put your ego aside, and look at what's really important for your family. It might seem impossible now, but with some time and effort, I know you can make it happen.

A cornerstone of a happy dual family is getting along with your ex on a day-to-day basis, instead of just some of the time. This is no easy feat. When deciding to end a marriage or partnership, there are deep and difficult emotions to take into consideration. It's likely you're hurt, and your heart and even your soul are deeply wounded. In addition to ourselves, we also have to think about our kids and their feelings and how our decisions affect them. We may also be taking our partner's feelings into account, and don't forget about other important people in your life, like close friends, family, siblings, and parents who may be very distraught over your decision to divorce. It's overwhelming! All this makes even thinking about getting along well with an ex that much more difficult, let alone actually making it happen. Don't worry, though. To help you along your path to success, I've included my personal secrets to creating a happy dual family and sustaining it day to day.

When dealing with your ex it's critically important to keep front of mind that how you choose to handle everyday situations will greatly affect the outcome of your dual family. This means sometimes taking the high road even when you know you're right, and it also means not taking the easy way out just to make things, well, easy momentarily. We create a lot of our own problems simply because we take the easy road instead of the harder but more appropriate road. Our decisions about how we choose to deal with the behavior of others have long-lasting implications as well. We all know those "spoiled brat" kids who have terrible manners, are rude to others, and yet still seem to get whatever they want. I hate to tell you, but they weren't born that way. They experimented with that behavior, and they got what they wanted. Years of reinforcement turns what could have been a perfectly lovely and polite child into the brat no one wants to be around.

So ask yourself: In your relationship with your ex, are you taking the easy way or the right way? Not only do you have to learn to deal with your ex and your kids the right way, but you also have to learn to deal with yourself the right way, too. Are you taking the easy way out in dealing with the bad behavior of your ex, your kids, or even yourself, or are you handling difficult situations head on and addressing issues before they get out of control? I've found that when I sweep an issue, nervous feeling, or a challenging person under the rug, I always regret it later on. Achieving a successful dual family means you first have to start dealing with *you* successfully. This is tough but so worth it and something you really can't avoid no matter how much you want to or how difficult it is for you to deal with. Being honest with yourself now will open you up to all the richness life has to offer. But you can only see the possibilities if you're very open and honest with yourself.

In fact, *you* play the key role in determining the success of your dual family. You can't change your ex's behavior, thoughts or plans, but you are in complete control of your own actions, thoughts and reactions. Even though, at times, you may feel out of control, you can learn to gain control quickly so you're able to do the right thing and handle tough situations in a cooperative way more often than not.

Remember, this process is about you, not your ex. It's about digging deep and discovering all the nasty things about you that, quite frankly, you might want to change, and to explore all the wonderful things that you want to express more. It's about learning what you want, what makes you happy, and how to create more of that in your life. It's about how to have the best relationship possible with your kids and enjoy life with them like you never have before, without all the family drama and difficulty. It's about designing your life and your family to be just the way you want. It took me a while, but I designed my life and my family just the way I wanted it, and I'm incredibly happy. I very much want that for you, too.

When I tell people about my unique relationship with my ex, I am frequently asked, "How did you do it? How do you keep it going?" The answer isn't simple, and it isn't short. I had to write a book to answer it. When I first got divorced and for years afterwards, I worked through a process to deal with my emotions, see the errors of my ways, realize what was really important to me, and then figure out how to get it. I wasn't conscientiously going through this process. As luck would have it, it just kind of happened. It wasn't until I was asked to write this book and people questioned how I got to where I am now that I really thought about it. I had to ask myself, What did I do? How did it all happen? Is there a step-by-step process that just about anyone could follow to create a happy dual family? There is! Part 1 of this book discusses the three-step process I went through. Everything I did may not work for you, but keep an open mind. You might be pleasantly surprised at what you can accomplish.

Once you've worked through the process, you must be cautious.

Introduction

If you're not careful, there are obstacles divorced couples face that can derail your happy family. In Part 2, I'll show you how to overcome what I consider to be the big three.

I've been focused on making my dual family work for many years now. That kind of success doesn't come easily, and every now and then I fall off the wagon. In Part 3, I share with you my secrets to keep myself in check and keep our family united and happy. Remember, don't dismiss these without trying them. If you say this won't work for you, before you even give it a try, you may miss out on some tools that may truly help you.

I understand my family is a little unusual in the way we all get along so well, but I believe happiness is possible for many divorced families. The tools and examples for helping divorced families get along just aren't widely available, and happily divorced families still aren't common. While I believe happiness is achievable for many, I realize this option isn't in the cards for some. If you're dealing with an ex who you have tried for years to get along with, and it just isn't happening, there's still hope for you. In Part 4, I've included an incredible story of happiness and strength in the face of some very difficult circumstances to show that even in the worst of times, you can work toward happiness and achieve the life of your dreams.

As I said before, this book is more about you than your ex, and it's your time to shine! You have the world at your feet and a chance for a new beginning. What are you going to do with this opportunity? In Part 4, I'll also show you how to design the life you want so you can live the life of your dreams. It isn't easy. But if you give it time and put your heart and soul into the process and really commit to creating a happy dual family for you and your kids, you likely will.

Think of this book as a guide to help you make over your family and set yourself on the right path after divorce. This is my story of struggles and aha moments that led me on a journey to becoming a better ex-wife, a better parent, and a better person after my divorce. By reading and learning from my stories and working through the exercises in the book, I hope to spare you some of the difficulties I faced and help you move on to becoming a happier family a little more quickly.

Stop and focus on each part of the book, taking as much time as needed to complete the exercises. You'll want a journal to write down your thoughts as you move through the exercises and record the areas of your relationship you want to grow and develop. I've also included my "Dual Family Steps to Success" at the end of each chapter to remind you what you can do right now to help you and your family move forward to a happier, healthier place.

Along the way, you'll see references to my website, www. DualFamily.com, where you'll find worksheets to help you with some of the exercises in the book. Just go to www.DualFamily. com/book-resources, then register to download the worksheets— and they're yours! You'll also find videos and seminars that dive deeper into the issues discussed in the book, with additional examples and more insight to help you discover more about yourself and how to create a happy family after divorce.

Introduction

Remember, I'm not a therapist, a doctor, or a marriage and family counselor. The process I outline was my personal path to emotional recovery. You'll likely have your own, so don't stop with these steps if you feel you need more help dealing with the emotional side of your divorce. It may be a good idea to seek the assistance of a therapist. I believe that if you're carrying around a lot of emotions about your ex or the loss of your marriage, you should work through them as much as possible, and a good professional can help. It's very difficult to move forward if you're emotionally tied to your past.

Don't lose faith. You can't control your ex and what he or she does, but you can certainly take charge of your own actions and how you deal with situations. You can teach your kids the ways of a loving, close family, whether you live under one roof or two, and you can have an incredibly happy life for yourself because you will have designed your life just the way you want it.

Are you ready? Turn the page and let's get started!

PART 1

The Process

"The turning point in the process of growing up is when you discover the core strength within you that survives all hurt."

—MAX LERNER

Years ago when I would speak with people about how well I get along with my ex and how happy our family is, I was almost always asked how I was able to make this happen. They wanted to do the same thing and have the same kind of success. They wanted an instruction manual on how to get along with their ex and make their divorced family happier. I didn't have an answer for them at that time; there wasn't a manual. It was through writing this book that I had to think about how I was able to move through the darkest feelings and emotions about my relationship and my ex and get to a place where I actually liked him again and we could work together as parents to support our son instead of bickering, fighting, and avoiding each other. It was through writing this book and lots of reflection that I realized I had gone through a process. I wasn't even aware it was happening, but I see it clearly now and I have outlined it for you here.

The process of creating a happy dual family and a happier you is likely to take some time. It was a few years before I had made big steps forward and began building not only the family I wanted, but the type of relationship I wanted with my ex. You'll have your own timeframe. It might be short and only take a few months, or it may take years. The timing of the process and how long it takes you to move through each step is not as important as knowing that it's a process. It's not going to happen all at once, and you must really sit with each part of the process and work through it completely to reap the rewards. Don't try and rush it because it's unpleasant or difficult. If you do, you'll be cheating yourself. Remember what I said earlier about not taking the easy way out. This is where it all starts.

The Process

I believe the steps I've outlined here are the most critical. You may find you need to add something to them, but please don't delete from them. It's easy for us to flip to the next page if we don't like something we're reading. No one will ever know, right? But you will know, and believe me, it will make a difference. No matter how difficult this is, you have to do it to come through on the other end. You don't have to dive into it full speed. Take baby steps if you need to, but keep moving forward.

It's important to know too that the steps are likely to overlap. That's totally expected. The first step is dealing with your grief. I don't know that my grief will ever completely go away. I still carry a little bit of it with me, but I worked through it to the point that I understood it, where it came from, and what role I played in it. I was finally able to resign myself to it and not hate myself for separating my family and was able to forgive myself and move on to have a great life and a loving dual family.

You may also find that you move some of these steps around a bit. That's alright too. This isn't rocket science after all. You're a unique individual and are most likely going to go through this process differently than I did. Just be sure to move through all of them completely. No skipping or shortcuts allowed.

Some people find it hard to believe they can actually get along well with their ex. They think it's a nice idea but a little pie in the sky. If you're still fuming mad at your ex, it might be difficult to find even one tiny reason that you would want to have any more to do with your ex than you absolutely have to. If you find yourself in this camp, you might need a little extra incentive, a little motivation to get you on your way to starting the process of a happy dual family.

Sometimes you have to see something to believe it. You need to create a vision for your new dual family. It's your motivation for what you do in your family relationship and how you handle situations. It's a mission statement of sorts and your ideal vision of your life and family, and it will absolutely help keep you on the right track throughout many, many years of dealing with your ex and your dual family. We'll talk more about creating your vision for your family later because you probably need to work through some issues before you can successfully construct it. For now just keep it in the back of your mind. I didn't have an idea of what I wanted my new family to look like for a couple of years after my divorce. I needed to go through the process so I could see the possibilities and visualize how great it would be if we all could get along and be happy together.

I fall back on my vision regularly now. It's my self-check system, and you won't believe how much trouble it keeps me out of. It's fantastic! Your vision for your family after divorce, how you want your family to be and interact on a day-to-day basis, will continue to guide you through the difficult times you are certain to have. So just start to think about it if you can, but it's not critical right now. What is critical now is that you start moving through the process. Remember, you have to give yourself to this. Grab a journal where you can write down your feelings and thoughts as you transition into your new life. Don't back off when it gets really hard. Just keep pushing forward, even when you don't want to. You'll face a lot of challenges and roadblocks throughout this process, but you have to stay the course. Remember, no shortcuts!

Before we begin, it's important to address one more critical issue. This is a time for you to deal with your emotions and thoughts in the most constructive way possible. You're working toward creating a better, more positive life for yourself and your kids. If you have people in your life who are negative, even if it's your best friend or a family member, please don't involve them in this process. They'll hinder you, and you'll question yourself far more if you allow their negative thoughts to affect you. We know they mean well when they say things like "That jerk of an ex of yours. Why in the world are you cutting him any slack?" They're just trying to show their support for you by being in your camp. Being in your camp is great, but we're trying to tear down walls here, not reinforce them. You might want to tell your friends and family that your intention is to create a mutually respectful and caring relationship with your ex so you can have a successful dual family for yourself and your kids. Ask them for their support by being positive and not making negative comments about your ex.

It should also be clearly understood that there should be an absolute restriction for everyone on bad mouthing your ex in front of your kids. Saying anything nasty or negative about your ex in front of your kids—even within earshot—is not OK. It can be very damaging to children to hear their parent being talked about that way. Not to mention the fact that it causes a lot of resentment and ill will when your kids reiterate to your ex that they heard your best friend, dad, sister, or whoever say he was a deadbeat or a loser or any other choice words you care to insert. The nasty comments always seem to find their way back to the person being talked about, and kids are notorious for blurting out those kinds of things. Set the right example for everyone and have a zero-tolerance policy against talking badly about your ex. You and your kids will be better off for it now and in the long run.

Making a dual family work after divorce is not always easy, especially in the beginning. Surrounding yourself with very supportive and positive people right now will help you to see the light at the end of the tunnel—and believe me, there is one. Stay away from the nasty negative and surround yourself with the perpetually positive.

We're ready to start step one. Get your tissues out. You'll need them. The first step is grieving.

CHAPTER 1

Grieving

"Grief does not change you. It reveals you."
—JOHN GREEN

This isn't pretty, but it's a critical step in the process to creating a happy dual family and making a fantastic life for you and your children. You have to thoroughly experience the grieving process so you can get past the anger, frustration, blame, and nastiness that so often plague divorced couples. This is the first step in being able to put the past behind you and not hate your ex, at least not completely. You may never get to the point where you're able to be great friends with your ex, but you have to purge the nastiness of the divorce, your negative feelings toward your ex and your circumstances so you can see your ex in a different and better light. I don't believe you can truly have a happy dual family without that, so don't hold back on your grieving!

This may take a while, and that's just fine. You can continue to grieve and still move forward with the rest of the process, but you should try to spend some time here before you attempt to move forward. Your progress may be stunted if you haven't worked through your grief enough and you still have a large amount of anger, frustration, and guilt, so just focus for a while on dealing with this.

When your marriage ends, so do all of your dreams and hopes for your life with your spouse or partner. This isn't easy to come to terms with. For me, the loss of the *idea* of my family was almost as bad as the actual loss itself. Grant and I were married for many years before we had a baby. When Evan finally came into our lives, I had wonderful visions of all the beautiful memories we would create as a family. Christmas is my favorite time of the year, and I relished the idea of waking up early with my husband on Christmas morning to set out all the gifts to surprise our little toe-headed toddler and watching with delight as he opened them up. It was a sweet thought that I focused on often while I was pregnant. We did have one lovely Christmas together as a family but we didn't make it to two. That first Christmas without my husband and my family together was brutally defeating. Honestly, the whole first year was. I don't think I've ever questioned myself so much or cried so often. I felt tremendous guilt because I was the one who wanted out of the marriage. I was unhappy in my relationship with my husband and just wanted it to end and saw divorce as the only way out.

I was fortunate enough to have an amazing support system of family and friends that rallied around me and helped me through it. At my lowest points—and there were many—they picked me up, dusted me off, loved me, and pulled me through. I hope you have a great support system you can turn to for love and encouragement. If you don't, try to find one, whether it's someone who can just be a sounding board or a therapist or a friend. Whatever you do, you should not rely on your children to be your support system. They need you to support them now. As you help to guide them into their new family life, they'll support you back in the form of love and affirmation, but we should never involve our children in our darkest times. They aren't equipped to deal with that. You always have to be the strongest one in the house. Not easy to do when inside you feel like a broken mess, but nonetheless, you must.

What does it mean to grieve fully, deeply, completely? For me, it meant I didn't have a tear left to cry and I was so spent from dealing with my loss that I had nowhere to go but up. Like a junkie on crack, I needed to hit bottom first. It was raw and deep and ugly for about a year. It was by far the most difficult year of my life, but I got through it, and so can you. It means you have to go with your feelings as you have them and express them when you can. Don't push them under the rug, don't try to be tough and hide your feelings or cover them up. Let it all out, as often as you need to, without involving the kids, for as long as you need to. I climbed out of my dark canyon after about six to nine months, and by the end of the first year, I had made real progress.

Let the grief out and move forward. Don't try to hide your feelings of loss, despair, fear, guilt, loneliness, or whatever else you may be feeling. Don't cover up the parts that are uncomfortable or that you want to gloss over and not deal with. Cutting corners now will not help you in the long run. We're not looking for quick fixes here, so put the time and work into it now, and you will reap the rewards down the road.

Speaking of quick, speed isn't important, but this process feels crappy, and I don't know about you, but I don't want to feel crappy any longer than I have to. So don't be afraid to hit it hard and let it out. Your journal can be of tremendous help here. Writing down your feelings and thoughts, no matter what they might be, is a freeing experience and always made me feel more in control. After my writing sessions I felt as though a weight had been lifted off of me, and I felt slightly calmer and more at peace.

You can use just about anything for a journal, whether it's a notepad or a bound book of blank pages. If you haven't journaled before, don't worry. It doesn't take any special skill. You're simply writing down your thoughts and feelings in one place. It's helpful to put the date on the pages when you write so you can go back and look at your thoughts at a particular time and track your progress. You'll want to use a journal throughout the book to catalog your answers and ideas.

I'm a fairly strong, self-reliant person, and I usually keep my innermost thoughts and emotions to myself. There are only a few very close and trusted friends in my inner circle that I am comfortable sharing my deepest emotions with freely. I rely on them for emotional support and help. Generally, I don't like to ask for help but will gladly accept it if it's offered. Dealing with my raw emotions and the end of my nine-year marriage was different though. I knew I couldn't do this on my own. I had to rally the troops for support. Leaning on my friends, I mean *really* leaning, was hard for me, but it helped tremendously. It was a life-changing experience that has stayed with me and made it much easier for me to ask for help and lean on others now. Having one or two people you can turn to, ask advice, use their shoulder as a tissue, or just vent to is an immense help and will assist you in moving through the grieving process.

There are some things, however, no one can help you with. You have to go through them on your own. This is where the raw emotions meet the deep grieving. My darkest moments were those I went through alone. But it was those same moments that propelled me forward and eventually out of the grieving process and closer toward my happy dual family.

When my husband and I separated, I was actually excited to move out of our family home and have my own place. For the very first time in my life, at 29, I would be on my own. My first couple of years in college I lived at home, then with a roommate in a dorm room on campus, and then with my fiancée who would later be my husband. I had never truly been on my own. I looked at our divorce as freedom, to not have to answer to anyone for once, and to do whatever I wanted whenever I wanted. I would be truly independent for the first time in my life. It was exciting to think about. But you know that saying, "be careful what you ask for because you just might get it"? That fit this situation perfectly. I was excited during the moving process and to spend the first few days and nights in my new home with Evan. Everything was great, we settled in, unpacked, played, got into a routine, had everything set up just right. We were enjoying our new home, and I was enjoying my freedom and not having to worry about the pressure of living in a failing marriage. Things seemed pretty good. I loved that Evan was there with me. He was my company and my focus. I had my baby with me, and I felt like nothing could be wrong when we were together. Up until that point, I had only been away from him a few days since he had been born. I stayed home with him and didn't work for the first year and a half of his life. We were together constantly. But now that Grant and I were living in separate places, his dad needed his time with Evan, too. It was that first night without Evan that took me to the lowest point I had ever been. I had some dark moments after that night, but nothing quite as desperate as this.

After three days in our new home, it was time for Evan to spend some time with his dad. We had agreed to meet in the parking lot of a store an equal distance from where we both lived. We were living about 15 minutes from each other at that point. We thought it would be easier for Evan if we did it that way rather than him being picked up and taken from one of his homes. It wasn't—for him, or for me.

I had everything prepared and ready. I packed his little lovey, an adorable stuffed animal that we called Bun Bun. It was the little white bunny from the *Pat the Bunny* book. Bun Bun was just as soft as he could be, and Evan carried it everywhere with him. I mean everywhere. It was rarely out of his sight, and he could not sleep without it. He also needed his robie. It was a red, silk sleep shirt of mine that he loved to rub in between his pudgy little thumb and index finger. Bun Bun and robie were his constant companions, and he needed both to soothe him to sleep. I was concerned about him sleeping at dad's house because he almost always slept with me and had a hard time getting to sleep and staying asleep if I tried to put him in his crib. I didn't know how Grant was going to handle sleep time, so I was a bit anxious. I just wanted my baby to be happy and comfortable. So, with Bun Bun, robie, and a few other favorite things in tow, off we went to meet Dad so Evan could spend a couple of days with him.

I often think how amazingly trusting kids are. Do you ever think about that? Ponder this for just a moment. Kids go wherever with us without question. They don't know if you're taking them somewhere dangerous or safe, to meet good people or bad people, to do something scary or fun; they just go, without question, and they are subjected to whatever you do to or with them. That's a very vulnerable place to be, with literally no power of their own, other than their voice. My baby trusted me to not harm him, to keep him happy, and to keep him safe. When he realized what was happening, he used his voice to tell me he wasn't happy about it.

We met Dad in the parking lot. Evan was perfectly happy as we pulled up and smiled when he saw his daddy. I unbuckled him from his car seat and cradled him in my arms as I pulled him out of the car. He always loved to be held. He grabbed onto me tightly as I got his Bun Bun, robie, and other things out of the car and handed them off to Dad. I wanted to hold on to Evan as long as I could, so I gave Grant everything else first as I reminded him of Evan's schedule. "Now, he goes to bed around 8 o'clock, and he needs to have a bottle before that. And don't forget he has to have Bun Bun and robie, too. I packed his favorite food. Do you have plenty of diapers?" "Yes, yes," Grant said. "I know all that. Don't worry. He'll be fine."

I wasn't convinced. I was growing more nervous by the second.

My heart started to pound faster as Grant walked over to us, gathered Evan's bag of goodies, and put Evan's things inside his car. The reality was setting in. I wasn't going to be with Evan for a couple of days. It seemed like an eternity. I got a knot in the pit of my stomach. I took a deep breath. "Time to go with daddy," I said. I could tell Evan still wasn't quite sure what was happening. With his arms wrapped around my neck, I pulled him away and handed him off to Grant. I stood there, just trying to take it all in. It was only a few seconds before he started to cry. Actually it was more like a wail. He screamed as Grant started to put him into his car seat. I ran to the car to try and calm him down. I reached out to touch him and said, "It's OK baby. Mommy's here. I love you. You're just going home with daddy." His face was red as he screamed, "Mommy, mommy" and reached his little arms out for me for me as if to say, "Get me out of here!" I felt like my baby was being tortured, and it was my fault!

Yes, I wanted the divorce, but I didn't want this. I didn't want Evan to be miserable. To see my baby hurting and so vehemently unhappy was just unbearable. Evan loved his dad and realistically, I knew he'd be fine, but I'd never been in this kind of situation before, and this wasn't a logical moment. It was pure emotion, fear, dread, and guilt. I tried to calm him, but it didn't work. Still screaming, he pulled at the straps on his car seat to try to get out. Grant suggested I just leave and that he'd calm down in a few minutes. That made sense, but what I really wanted to do was grab him and take him back home with me and try again another day. Grant shut the door with Evan still crying at the top of his lungs. It would have been better and probably easier for me if I had just gotten in my car and left. But watching Evan and the anxiety he was going through was like watching a train wreck. I couldn't take my eyes off of him. No parent wants to see their baby in pain, but it's even worse to walk away and leave them. I just couldn't do it. I watched, heartbroken, as they drove away.

I stood there, stunned, finally able to break down now that Evan was out of sight. I got into my car and had my own crying fit. I cried all the way home and couldn't get the sight of my very unhappy baby out of my head. I felt horrible. I had made him unhappy. I had put him in this situation. For the very first time it hit me. *This* was going to be my life. What the hell had I done? I started to panic. Not only had I ended my marriage, but I made my baby, the person I loved most, miserable. He was so used to being with me. Would he be happy with his dad? Would he be alright in the house if I wasn't there? What if Grant didn't watch him or play with him as much as I did? I didn't have any answers. My head was racing, and my heart was sick.

I was only slightly calmer by the time I got home to the apartment I rented. That didn't last long though. I walked into an empty house for the first time in about 10 years. I was completely overwhelmed by emotions. My marriage was over, my baby was miserable, and I was alone. This wasn't what I wanted. This was not how I planned it. I wanted to be happier, not unhappier! The empty house made everything worse. I was sick to my stomach. I frantically paced around the house looking for something to do, something to distract me. There was nothing! I had lost everything: my home, my husband, my baby, my family, I didn't even have my dog with me. Guilt took over me. What kind of a person does this? I thought to myself. I laid down on my bed and cried. I grabbed a pillow, curled up, and just let it go. I cried so hard, I could barely breathe. I had never felt this much pain, guilt, and anguish before. It was horrible. I knew this was going to be one hell of a night.

I was missing Evan terribly. Grant and I had agreed on 50/50 custody. How in the world would I be able to live half the time without him? It didn't seem possible. Then I started questioning my decision to get a divorce. My mind jumped frantically from thought to thought. Maybe we should get back together. Maybe we just didn't try hard enough. If we went to counseling again, maybe that would work! I was willing to do just about anything to make this misery go away and have my little boy back. I missed his smiles and laughs and the way he giggled when I tickled him. I missed cuddling and watching his favorite movies with him. I missed the way his eyes lit up when I read his special books to him. I missed running my fingers through his silky blonde hair and kissing his soft skin. I missed everything about him!

I knew that I would be away from him regularly for many years to come. How could I do that? As thoughts of him poured through my head, my pain and anguish turned to desperation. I panicked! I needed to have some part of him, now! I needed something that was his. I knew I had already given all his favorite things to his dad but I searched anyway. I looked in the living room for a favorite toy I could hold, but there was nothing there. I looked for a stuffed animal that might be lying around. I found nothing. I went to the bedroom, looked under the bed, nothing. I ran out to the car in hopes of finding something there, the closet, the bathroom. I was growing more desperate by the minute.

I know this is going to sound bizarre, but I thought, if I could only smell him. Yes, that was it! His smell! Finally, I had a glimmer of hope to find something that would connect me to my baby! I had just changed the sheets on the bed so the pillows were no help. I ran to the dresser in the bedroom, knelt down in front of it and opened every drawer. I frantically pulled out every piece of his clothing so I could smell them. I knelt on the floor with high hopes as I grabbed each piece of clothing and inhaled deeply. Everything was just too clean. I couldn't smell him at all! I grew desperate again and went to the bathroom to look for a towel or something there. Again, everything was clean. Damn it! Where is he, I said to myself. Then it hit me: the laundry basket! There were a few pieces I hadn't washed yet. I ran to the closet, grabbed the basket and hurled its contents onto the floor. I threw aside the few pieces of my clothing and what remained was all I had left of my baby that night. Desperate and broken, I quickly collected them into a ball, held them close to my chest and took a deep, long breath. There he was. His scent on a bundle of cold, lifeless clothes brought him back to me. I could smell my baby! I finally had a tiny piece of him with me.

As strange as it may seem, that ball of dirty clothes was a huge comfort to me. It was literally all I had that night of my son who I loved so much. I gathered the clothes up and lay down on the bed. I didn't try to mask my feelings or be tough. I just went with it and let all the desperation, fear, anguish, and guilt just come out. I must have cried off and on for a couple of hours before I finally fell asleep, exhausted, miserable, spent.

I didn't expect to have this degree of emotions, nor had I

anticipated regretting my decision to get divorced so much. As I lay there curled up on the bed, desperately hugging this ball of dirty baby clothes, now wet from my steady stream of tears, I thought to myself, Will this pain ever go away? How long will it take for me to feel normal again? Will I feel normal again? Will Evan be OK? What is this going to do to him? Will he remember this? The questions just kept coming, and I didn't have a single answer. This was a horrible place to be, but there was nowhere else for me to go.

Remember when I said before that you have to relinquish yourself to this part and allow yourself to fully grieve? As hard as it is, you must do that. Don't try to put a pretty face on it. Don't try to smooth it over and put it aside. It won't get better that way. Allow yourself to experience all the ugliness. It's such a miserable place to be, but being there fully and completely and getting it out of your system will allow you to be able to move on and pick up the pieces down the road. Putting up a false front for yourself or anyone else isn't going to help you now or later on. Spend some time alone with your thoughts and emotions and get it all out.

The next morning I didn't feel much better. I had woken from the worst night of my life. My head was pounding from all the intense emotion, stress, and lack of sleep, and my eyes were swollen from hours of crying. I had never experienced anything of that depth before and I never wanted to again. If there was a hell on earth, I had been in it. All the thoughts from the night before slowly started to creep back in as I woke up and my heart began to beat nervously again. I was thinking slightly more logically now and decided to call Grant to see how Evan was doing. I had to know if he was OK. I anxiously picked up the phone and called, not knowing if I would hear crying, laughing, or nothing at all on the other end. To my surprise, he said he had a good night, slept well, and was happily playing. I didn't hear screaming in the background. Believe me, I was listening for it. So I figured he was probably right. As shocked as I was, I was incredibly relieved. As I hung up the phone and reflected on the calmness of the moment, I thought, maybe Evan would actually be alright through all of this. As I continued to think about that, I started to see a glimmer of light. If he's happily playing with his dad and had even slept well, then maybe I hadn't scarred him for life. Maybe he'll adjust and get used to this after a while. But will I adjust and get used to this? Only time would tell, but at least now I had a bit of hope.

I never had a night quite like that again, thankfully. I still cried a lot and had some rough patches for many months until we all started to adjust to our new lives. Like kids do, Evan adjusted quickly. He still had a little bit of a hard time when we handed him off to each other, but we experimented with different locations and ways of doing it until we came up with what worked best for him.

Little by little, I got used to having an empty house and I adjusted, although I was always happier when Evan was with me. After a while the empty house didn't feel so lonely anymore. I always missed having Evan home, but I was content knowing that he was able to be happy at his dad's house and they were able to share important bonding time together.

That first night, I was so frantic and distraught, but I had to go through it on my own. No one else could have pulled me through that or even comforted me; my emotions were too deep and painful. After that awful night, though, I started to rally my friends. A phone call to a trusted ally was a great comfort to me. Whether in person or on the phone, a shoulder to cry, on or an ear to bend was incredibly helpful and very cathartic.

I still had a lot to work through for many years after that, but it got easier. The deep grieving was a different story; I tried to work through it completely and quickly. I really don't like crying and being miserable, so I figured the sooner I dealt with all of it, the sooner I would lose the desire to cry anymore. I didn't try to hold back or cover it up. I didn't tell everyone I was fine, because I wasn't. They knew I was miserable. I was vulnerable and weak, and I was OK with that. I allowed myself to break down to my lowest point and then I started to build myself back up. That's what allowed me to begin my transition to the next step of the process: acceptance.

If we only explore the feelings we think make us right or feel better, we aren't growing. We're stuck in the same place we've been. Sorry to tell you, but if you haven't already figured it out, staying in the same place is not what this book is about. To be able to create a happy dual family for yourself and your kids, you have to change and grow. Get out all your grieving and deal with every piece of it so you can move to the next step and accept your new reality.

Think about what saddens you most about your relationship ending. What have you lost? Think not only of the physical things like a house, car, or family but the emotional things. Did you lose dreams, your best friend, your sense of control, or even self-worth? Are you grieving over the time you're losing with your kids, friends, or your in-laws? Make a list of all the things you feel a sense of loss over. How does losing these things make you feel? Take some time doing this and write it all down in your journal. Add to it daily as you realize all the different things in your life you may have lost or had to give up. Don't leave out anything, no matter how small. We're dealing with this in its entirety so it's less likely to come back and flare up on you later on.

As you're making your list and writing down how losing these pieces of your life makes you feel, you may experience frustration or anger and even fear. It's perfectly understandable why you would feel angry or fearful over the loss of friends or your home, your way of life, or anything you don't have anymore. Just as with the feelings of loss, don't push the anger or frustration under the rug. Allow yourself to get it out and experience it in a healthy and safe way. Write those feelings down in your journal and get them out.

A common coping technique in this kind of situation is to write a letter to your ex and tell them how angry you are about your divorce and the things you've lost. You will never actually send this letter, but it may make you feel better to write it and even put it in an envelope and address it. Just make sure you stash it somewhere safe where no one will find it. You could also write the letter in your journal.

However, if your anger or fear seems like it's getting the better of you and you're having a difficult time coping with it, you may want to see a therapist who can help you work through it more completely. The idea of dealing with the feelings of loss is not to dwell on them but to recognize them, deal with them, and move on so you're less likely to hold a grudge against your ex. It's awfully difficult to build a happy dual family when you're still holding on to anger, resentment, fear, or frustration towards your ex and your divorce. The more thoroughly you work through it, the more successful you'll be in cooperating with your ex to create a happy family.

Your new life and family situation is what it is. There's not much that can be done about it, but by grieving fully, you can begin to turn the losses and grief you feel into more positive emotions. You'll start to become more positive as you work through the other steps in the process.

Dual Family
STEPS TO SUCCESS

- ▸ Get a journal to use throughout the book.

- ▸ Make a list of everything you lost in your divorce, and write it down.

- ▸ If you feel anger, fear, or resentment, chronicle these feelings in your journal.

- ▸ To help you deal with your feelings, write a letter to your ex to tell them how you feel. Don't send the letter, and keep it in a safe place.

- ▸ Work with a therapist if you think you can't work through your feelings on your own.

Chapter 2

Acceptance

"Happiness can exist only in acceptance."
—George Orwell

Make no mistake, you don't just stop grieving and start accepting. This is a process that will morph in and out of different stages, and you'll likely be in one or more stages at the same time. Hopefully at this point, you've been able to get some deep grieving done, and you're starting to get a hold on where you are emotionally. You're likely starting to feel a little more normal and settling into your new unmarried life, and you're probably slightly more comfortable with your circumstances. Nights might still be a little lonely and you miss your kids terribly when they're gone, but at least you can deal with it now. You're moving toward acceptance.

Acceptance is more than just being satisfied with your new life. That's definitely part of it, but it's also about accepting what happened in your marriage so you don't hold a nasty grudge. It's about accepting the role you played in your marriage ending and, most important, accepting yourself. Acceptance was a long process for me. I had been with my husband for about 11 years. To now be alone for the first time in my life was so foreign. It seemed like at any minute he would come home and we'd talk about our day like we normally did. We'd cook dinner together, play with the baby, and have our normal evening. Of course, none of that happened.

Aside from the loneliness, I had to accept that I was now a divorced, single mother. That was something I had never intended to happen. I'm a romantic at heart and always wanted to grow old with my husband and have a long love affair. The problem was, the passion faded in our marriage, and we didn't know how to get it back. We didn't exactly take care of our love, either. We went on just two or three vacations together the entire time we were married. We were more concerned with our jobs and getting a great start in life financially than we were in each other and taking care of our relationship. Working, making money, saving money, and buying our homes seemed to take precedence over taking care of each other. We didn't take enough time to love and nurture each other and grow and bond together. I didn't realize the effect all this was having on us until it was too late. After almost a decade together, I loved my husband but as more of a friend than anything else. I had fallen out of love with him, and my passion was gone.

Going through acceptance can teach you so much about yourself if you take the time to focus on it, learn, and understand. I've learned some great things about me and some not-so-great things, too. I realized I'm a very passionate person, and I absolutely need passion in my relationship as well. Today, I understand much better what it takes to make that happen and keep it going. With each relationship I have I get closer to the deep, passionate, loving, fun relationship I want. That great relationship just wasn't in the cards for me and my husband. Accepting that was very tough. I wished many times that I would have seen things as they were and had been able to do something about it. Maybe if we had taken more vacations, put us first and not worried so much about getting ahead financially, we'd still be married. I questioned myself a lot the first year we were divorced. No matter how many questions I asked or how many answers I received, it wouldn't change the fact that my marriage was over. You can't go back and change the past. What happened in the past had happened, and now I was divorced. That was a hard pill to swallow for a girl who thought she'd live to a ripe old age with the love of her life. Accepting that was a huge hurdle for me and it took some time.

In this part of the process, not only do you have to accept your new reality of being divorced and how you got to that point, but you also have to accept where you are, literally. Grant and I owned our own home. I took great pride in my home and absolutely loved it. When I moved out, I left my 1,800-square-foot, beautiful custom home and moved into a 400-square-foot studio above someone's garage. Renting a home for the first time in 10 years and having it be so small felt like a huge step down for me. It was a cute little place and it had everything we needed, but it wasn't ideal. I couldn't have more than one or two people over at a time because there wasn't enough room. The living room was only about 150 square feet! It was tiny to say the least, but it was inexpensive. It was also located in an area I knew well. The familiarity of the neighborhood made me feel safe and it was comforting, but I missed my house, my yard, my garden, my dog, and all my things that wouldn't fit into my new 400 square feet.

I was talking with a friend of mine the other day and he mentioned some couples he knows who want to get divorced, but they just can't deal with letting the house go. They sleep in separate bedrooms and speak only when necessary. They're not happy together and are in a passionless marriage, but they just can't give up the house and the stuff. Really? I hope this doesn't describe you. Is a house, car, or furniture more important than your happiness? It shouldn't be. Those are just things and although they may be able to bring you some pleasure, they can't love you. For me, happiness comes from the love and connection I have with those who are closest to me. That's what comforts me, not the street I live on or the car I drive. Those material things aren't important, especially right now. The more energy and time you put toward keeping those things in your life, the less energy and time you have for you and your kids. Right now, you need to heal, and you must help your kids through this process as well. They need your guidance and love desperately right now; a house does not.

I could have fought my ex for the house. I loved that house. I wanted that house, believe me! But I had to really think about what was critically important to me now and over the next several years. The clearer I got about that, the less I thought about the house. I could have made an excuse to fight for the house and said that keeping it would help keep my son's life stable and he'd adjust better with us there. But I knew in my heart that Evan would be happy wherever we decided to live, and besides, it's my job to provide stability in his life. A house in and of itself doesn't create stability, the people inside it do. I knew my focus needed to be on rebuilding my life, getting a job, and raising my son. I didn't have a job when I left my marriage, so supporting myself, Evan, and a big house payment was unlikely. The stress of a large mortgage payment and all the bills that come along with the house wasn't exactly ideal, either. I knew I wouldn't have a lot of time for doing yard work or housework because Evan was still a baby, and he was the one who needed my attention, not concrete and wood. The more I thought about it and got very clear on what I wanted to focus on (Evan) and what was important to me (rebuilding a happy and successful life with him), the more the house became unimportant and I embraced the concept of living small. Grant kept the house.

Part of acceptance is also dealing with the problems in your relationship and what role you played in those problems. What got you to the point of divorce? Take out your journal again or download the "Acceptance Worksheet" from the Resources page at www.DualFamily.com and start creating a list of all the things that went wrong in your relationship. This is a time when you can grieve, get really mad at your ex, and let your emotions run free. You can even list all of the nasty things you feel your ex did. You have to get this out of your system to be able to move forward, but you can't move forward if you don't stop and look at where you've been.

There may have been cheating, emotionally, physically or both. There may have been an illness involved, drug or alcohol use, or some type of abuse. You may have simply grown in different directions or career and opportunities became more important than the marriage, or you simply fell out of love, or maybe you realized you never should have gotten married in the first place. I already mentioned that it was largely a lack of taking care of our relationship that led to my divorce. We allowed complacency to take over our relationship and our intimacy faded. It was compounded by other issues. Over the years we became more unloving and uncaring toward each other. We went through the day-to-day motions of married life, but there was no desire to make it sizzle, make it special. That is something that every relationship needs, especially a marriage. We simply didn't do it. By listing all the things I felt we had done wrong, I was able to face them, grieve for the marriage and family that I wanted and never got, deal with it and move forward. Make your list, acknowledge the reality of what has happened, get angry if you have to, and deal with it. Your wife may have cheated. Your husband may have left you. No matter what happened, at some point, you need to move forward and move on with your life. I know that may seem impossible now, but believe me, if you focus your energy in a more positive direction, you can do it; you'll be better off for it and so will your kids!

So you're on your way to accepting your new circumstances and what caused your relationship to break down. That's a lot to digest. This isn't a race so I hope you aren't moving through this too quickly. Without a guide or help this process took me years to work through. With the assistance of this book, you may be able to move through this process more quickly, but again, how long it takes isn't critical. What's most important is that you work fully and completely through each step and make sure you process it completely before you move on. So pause here for a moment and make sure you're really dealing with everything we've talked about. If you think you still need to grieve a little more, do it. If you still aren't comfortable with where you are in your life, connect with those you love the most and focus on you, your kids and building a fantastic and strong connection with them. And if you need to be mad at your ex a little more, do that, too. It's OK, really. I'm only going to let you do that for a little while longer though, so get it out now while you can because we'll be putting the kibosh on that pretty quickly.

Take some additional time here, a few weeks or months if you need to, and sit with what you've done so far. You've done some great work. Enjoy your progress! You deserve it! This is absolutely some of the hardest work you will ever do, but it's work that is life changing, and it will change you and your family forever if you do it right and you stick with it. When you're ready, let's move on to the next step of acceptance. Oh yes, there's more!

I hope you savored despising your ex for the last time, because the time has come: We're done with that now. Here comes the really fun part. You get to look at *you* now and discover the nasty, negative side of yourself that contributed to the end of your relationship. Ooooh, didn't see that one coming, did you? Sorry, but this is critical to your progress. Let's face it, no one likes to look inside at the less than desirable qualities we all have. You might be saying right about now, "But I'm an angel and such a good person, I honestly don't have any awful qualities." Sorry, but yes you do. Everyone does. If you want to blame it on something, blame it on your species. We're human. We have loads of faults, and it's exceedingly likely that you exhibited some of them in your marriage and it wasn't pretty. It's alright. I wasn't always at my best either, so you're in good company. It's time to be honest about what got you here in the first place. You have to man or woman up and admit what part you played in the demise of your relationship if you want to move forward.

Looking at yourself and your faults is never an easy task, especially in the emotionally charged environment you're in now, but you need to do it to be able to move on and not see your ex as the enemy. If you see your ex as the enemy, you can't have a happy dual family. Your ex will stay the enemy unless you can see your own faults and not blame your ex for everything. Having a more realistic view of the role you played in your marriage ending, instead of blaming your ex, will help you soften your approach with your ex and perhaps, in time, even want to get along. I often blamed my ex for all my unhappiness in the marriage. I've come to realize, though, that a large part of my unhappiness was my own fault. I didn't know that at the time, so it was easy for me to place the blame squarely on my husband.

I had been unhappy for the last few years we were married, but the last two years we were together were especially difficult. Perhaps the stress and pressure of a strained marriage with a baby on the way made him harsh. Whatever the reason was, I bore the brunt of some nastiness that I felt I didn't deserve. I felt I had no other option than to leave my loveless marriage where I was getting very few of my needs met. I blamed him for pushing me to that decision. I felt justified by that rationale. As long as I was feeling it was his fault and he was the bad guy, that made me right. It helped me sleep at night knowing that it was his fault. The problem is, that was *my* reality. There are two people in every marriage. Each person has their own view of what happened in the relationship, and it's quite possible, even likely, that these views differ greatly. You have your view and opinion, and your ex has theirs. And guess what? Both of you are right! Your view is right for you, and your ex's view is right for him. It isn't until we get some distance, some perspective, and we are big enough and strong enough to look inside ourselves at all the not-so-nice things we could have done differently, that we can begin to see the other's point of view.

We've covered a lot so far, so you might be saying, tell me again why I want to see my ex's perspective on anything? Well, it's because you are a wonderful person and loving parent who only wants the best for yourself and your children, and you know that holding a grudge against your ex won't benefit you or your kids in any way. The negative energy those feelings produce will inhibit you from developing the deepest bond you can possibly have with your kids, and it will prevent you from being your happiest, most successful self in life. Are those good enough reasons? Of course they are!

I had plenty of reasons to be angry at my ex. I didn't have my baby with me all the time anymore, I was living in a tiny studio, I had to go back to work, I lost my house, he didn't give me the love and care that I wanted, and don't forget, he was mean. At least, that was my opinion. I was completely disinterested in seeing his side. Honestly, I was so stuck in my own reality that I didn't think there could be any other way of looking at it. I admit that was a very self-absorbed view of life, but we get like that, don't we? Once we get stuck in that selfish mentality, it takes a bolt of lightning to knock us off our perch. Sometimes being struck by lightning, at least the hypothetical kind, is a good thing!

Grant and I were civil to each other after the divorce. We talked when necessary but not much more because there was still some anger on both sides. Grant wasn't always great with Evan's schedule and getting him back on time or picking him up on time. My bolt of lightning hit during a phone conversation centered around scheduling and "my time" and "his time" with our son.

Now, I'm going to be really big here and share with you a time when I was just a hair shy of perfect. If I can do this in a book for all to read, then you can do this with yourself and admit some of your own mistakes in your marriage. We all have them, but you have to admit them if you're going to truly heal, move on, and develop into a better you.

I called Grant to deal with a scheduling issue that had really irritated me. He had dropped off Evan late several times, and I had to constantly adjust my schedule on the fly. When he picked up the phone, I tore into him. The conversation went something like this: Me angrily saying, "Evan was supposed to be back here over an hour ago. Why haven't you called? You can't just drop him off whenever you want. I have things to do. When are you getting over here? You knew what the schedule was!"

Grant was silent on the other end for a moment. Then he spoke my lightning bolt. I remember it clearly. He snapped back at me very sternly and said, "You know, you can't just yell at me like that. If we're going to get along, we have to talk things through." The calmness in his voice and the obvious rationale of his words kind of threw me back. I was a little stunned. I didn't quite know what to say because he was right. Damn it! At this moment, I was still in the one point for me, one point for him mentality, and he had just scored a major point! Crap, there goes my winning streak! As I'm processing his words, I took a deep breath and said, "You're right. I'm sorry. I won't do that again. Ummmm, when do you think you can have Evan back here?"

I felt about two inches tall after that conversation, and it made me do some major thinking. If Grant was right about that, and I was wrong in speaking to him that way, and I'm sure I had spoken to him that way before, then what else had I been wrong about? Probably a lot of things. Oh no! Was I the one who ruined our relationship? I questioned myself, almost in a panic at this point. The answer? Sure I did. I had a big part in the demise of our relationship. Until this point, I could only see the wrong ways of my husband. How could adorable me do anything to wreak havoc on my marriage? Plenty, I'm sure. It's a darn good thing I didn't ask Grant for his opinion or you'd have some really good answers.

The point is to move forward; it's not important to keep score and figure who's right and who's wrong. The marriage is over, and it's extremely likely that two people (yes, that includes you) were involved in making that happen. Being able to see this and accept it is a tough task. We don't like to admit to the things in us that aren't so great. But let's face it, you can't improve those things if you don't admit to yourself what they are, and that maybe you should change them. You know the saying, "you can't change someone else." However, you can change yourself, but you have to want to do it first.

I didn't want to hold a grudge against my ex-husband. I was just angry that I didn't get the happy life I wanted, and I blamed it on him. But hanging on to that anger wasn't making me a better or nicer person, and it wasn't helping my son. It just made me angry. We can't cleanse our soul if it's full of anger. That's why the grief process is so important. Obviously, I was still harboring some resentment for Grant at this point. I needed to grieve some more and accept my new reality so I could be more comfortable in it. I wasn't quite there yet, even though I was getting more and more settled in my new life and becoming happier. I didn't want my son to grow up with his parents not getting along and never spending family time together. I loved him so much, I wanted him to always have the best of both of us. So I started to forgive Grant and more important, I started to forgive myself.

When I realized I had played a large role in the failure of my marriage, I had tremendous guilt. Not only had I been the one who wanted the divorce, but I realized I was a big part of the problem too. Wow! That was a lot to digest. I wasn't happy about this new realization, but I knew I had to deal with it. Accepting this was hard, but it allowed me to see Grant in a very different light. All of a sudden, he wasn't mean and he wasn't the bad guy who had caused poor little me so much pain. In fact, I started to feel bad for some of the things I had done over the years we were together.

I wished I had this insight when we were still married. Maybe if I had this awareness, then I would have been a little kinder, sweeter, more loving and understanding, and maybe we would have made it. But maybe we still wouldn't have. The truth is, we don't know why things happen the way they do sometimes, and we're just left to deal with it. How we deal with it, though, makes all the difference in the world.

Acceptance of your circumstances, where you are and what role you played in your marriage leading to a divorce, makes all the difference in the world, too. Being truly honest with yourself about your faults and your actions that may have led to your divorce, whether it was simply not carving out enough time for each other, being more friends and not lovers and friends, being mean and nasty too often, and being honest about anything else that may have happened will help you move past it. It's not fun, it's not easy, but it is necessary, and if you have any intention of creating a happy dual family, you must do this.

So, before we go any further, take out your journal and write down a list of everything you can think of, big or small, that you could have done in your relationship to get you to where you are now. C'mon, you know what I mean. The snide comments, being unsupportive of something your partner wanted to do, not listening, not respecting your partner's wishes, being a little too caught up in your own activities instead of creating activities for the two of you to do together. Were you too focused on your career, or did you cheat? It can be a long list if you work at. Be sure to write down everything you can think of, the big and the little things.

The point of this exercise is not to make you feel bad. We aren't perfect. We make mistakes every day, and that's totally fine, we're supposed to, it's in our nature. It's those mistakes we make on a regular basis that tear down our relationship and prevent us from creating a truly happy life with our partner that we need to focus on here. If you throw your underwear and towels on the floor instead of the hamper like my ex did, although he'll swear to this day that it never happened, as undesirable as that is, it probably didn't break up your marriage. Being uninterested and unsupportive of the dreams and goals of your spouse, however, may have played a role in it.

Remember, this is an opportunity for you to look inward, not outward to your ex. You're not starting a his-and-her-bad-things list. I know, that stinks, but we're growing into better people, right? We're trying to bury the hatchet, not chop more wood for the fire. You're going through the process of letting go of the anger you have from all the things your spouse did and looking at what role you played. If it makes you feel better, write a list of the wonderful things you did in your marriage, too. And since we're growing and becoming better people, you can make a column on that good-things list for your ex, too. At least put down one or two. I promise it's a positive thing to do and might just make you feel a little bit better about your ex. You can write all this down in your journal, or you can download the "Acceptance Worksheet" on the Resources page at www.DualFamily.com/book-resources.

At this point you might be asking, Why am I putting myself through all this again? We're moving on to step three, and it makes all this hard work you've been doing much, much easier.

Dual Family
Steps to Success

- Get out your journal or simply download the "Acceptance Worksheet" on the Resources page of www.DualFamily.com/book-resources.

- Write down all the things that went wrong in your marriage. List everything that contributed to your breakup.

- Include specifically the mistakes you made.

- So you end on a happier note, write down all the wonderful and loving things you did in your marriage, and write down a few for your ex as well.

Chapter 3

Creating Your Vision for the Future

"We are limited, not by our abilities,
but by our vision."
—Unknown

It's easy to get discouraged in this process. There's a lot of difficult work to do, and you've done quite a bit already with the grieving you've worked through, learning about yourself and what role you played in your relationship ending, and hopefully starting to see your ex in a new and better light. It may seem like all you're doing is dealing with negative emotions right now, but don't give up. You're starting to get to some of the good stuff! It's so much easier to stay on course if you have a plan. A vision, if you will. The reasons you're here and why you want a happier and better life for you, your children, and your family. You may have been thinking a little bit about that already, and this is where you're going to dive into it and explore more of what you want from your new family and why.

What made going through the process easier for me was gazing at my beautiful little boy and knowing how much he would benefit from all my efforts. I still sometimes sneak into his room and watch him as he sleeps. I'll sit next to him on the bed and gently touch his hair and his sweet little face as I watch him breathe. Man I love him! As many parents are, I am selfless with him. I want him to have the best of everything. That includes the best of me and his dad. If I only wanted him to have the best of me and not his dad, then that would be very selfish and not truly loving at all, wouldn't it? If our son was going to have the best of us, that meant we had to be at our best, and for me that meant I had to be able to see the best in my ex. If you can't see something good in your ex, it's too easy to turn to the dark side and begin to sabotage your child's relationship with him or her. You may not mean to do it intentionally, but it happens. We're human, and we tend to do things like that. If you're still harboring some resentment and haven't fully moved through steps one and two of the process, this can more easily happen.

It might start with a little comment that you don't think has too much impact, but to your child, it could be devastating. Let's say your ex is frequently late picking up your kids. When your ex is late for the third time in a row, and your child says, "Where's daddy?" you might return the question with something like "Well, looks like your dad is late *again!* I'm never late picking you up because you're so important to me. I guess that means I love you more." I hate to admit it, but I used to say little comments like this. Not often, usually when Grant had made me really mad and before I had fully moved through the process. Sometimes it happened without me even thinking about it. When I look back at it, I feel terrible. It was very selfish of me and not at all loving toward my son. The intention with that kind of a comment might be to make your ex look bad, but what does it really do? It makes your beautiful child, the one you adore more than anything else in the world, feel inferior in the eyes of the other parent. That is never acceptable to do.

My job as a parent is to set the right example for my child and teach him how to behave in the world so he grows up to be the best person he can be. If I'm making snide remarks about his dad, how is he learning to behave? He's learning that it's acceptable to speak poorly about someone else, even a family member. That certainly wasn't my intention, but that's what was happening. Even worse, I may have made my child feel that he was unimportant to one of the most critical people in his life, his father. That wasn't intentional, either, but nonetheless, it was terribly wrong. I'm telling you this so you'll hopefully recognize this type of behavior when it presents itself and you can put an end to it quickly and for good.

Much of this whole process is about self-awareness, so you're more likely to see when you're headed in the wrong direction or down the wrong path and away from what your ideal vision is for your new dual family. When you have clarity and are aware of what you're doing and why and you focus on that vision regularly, you make the right decisions more frequently and are more likely to have happy, secure kids, be happy yourself, and have a happy dual family.

Your vision is what step three is all about. It's kind of like your big why. What's the reason you want to have a happy family after divorce? How do you want your kids to feel about you, your ex, and your changed family? How do you want everyone to interact?

Think about what you want your dual family to look and feel like on a day-to-day basis. This can actually be kind of fun if you have the right attitude. If you thought you were ruining your kid's life by getting a divorce, here's your chance at redemption! How great is that?

Jim Rohn, the motivational speaker and author, said, "Happiness is not an accident nor is it something you wish for. Happiness is something you design." I love that quote because he's absolutely right! You can't just hope your divorce turns out OK, you can't wish that your kids are happy; you have to plan it out, step by step, and then follow through to ensure it happens, and when it gets off track, because trust me, it will, you have a plan to pull it back in the right direction. You're directing the new circumstances of your family.

I didn't want my son to grow up with his mom and dad fighting over him and feeling that he's being pulled in two different directions, not wanting to hurt or play favorites with either one of us, having to second-guess himself on what he really wants to do just so he doesn't hurt our feelings. That's a lot of pressure and stress for anyone, especially a child, and it can prevent them from being who they really are. They have to be what you want them to be or what they think you want them to be instead. That's no way to raise a child.

I started to notice how happy Evan was when Grant and I were getting along and took the time to visit with each other for a few minutes on the days we exchanged him. Some peaceful chatting turned into a few minutes of the three of us playing together and eventually lunch or dinner and more time together. Evan was so happy to have us all together as a family. From his perspective, there was no reason we shouldn't be a family even though we were divorced. And you know what? He was right.

When I took some time and really thought about what I wanted my family to look like after divorce, it was something like this:

- Evan will never feel he has to choose between me and his dad.
- Grant and I will openly discuss any issues we have as a family.
- Evan's birthday and some holidays will be spent together as a family.
- Grant and I will equally share in the responsibility to raise Evan and discuss important issues that affect him like illnesses, school, sports, etc.
- Evan will feel completely comfortable and safe at each of our homes.
- Our family unit will always comes first and is our priority.
- Keeping the peace in our dual family will be paramount.
- We will all work together to keep the family unit cohesive and happy.
- We will attend Evan's school and sporting events together as a family.
- We will continue to do fun things as a family like go to movies together and have dinner together.
- Evan will always be secure in our love for him so he can focus on being a kid, growing up, learning, and having fun.

- Grant and I will always feel comfortable coming over to each other's homes and calling to speak with Evan.
- We will be supportive of each other and work through our differences and issues with care and respect toward each other.

Those were just some of the main points of my vision, but they give you an idea of where I was going. I wanted a happy, loving, communicative, cooperative, supportive family that just happens to live in two different homes. Oh sure, we started out the way most divorced couples do: playing the "this is my time, that's your time," "this is my role, that's your role" game; arguing about what rules to impose on Evan and disciplinary issues, but that gets really old after a while. It's such a negative way to exist, and you can't grow as a person or as a family if you're constantly bickering and arguing or if you see your ex as the enemy or someone whom you have to put up with.

Seeing your ex as someone who's cooperative, helpful, a great parent to your child, and communicates with you in an open, positive way not only makes your family life much easier, but it makes your whole life easier! When your life is easier, you have more energy and time to create the exciting, passionate, fun life you've always wanted! Isn't that cool? Are you getting where this is all going? As I've said throughout this book, it's not just about your divorce; this is about living life in the best way you can. But you have to do the work to get to the point where you can see all the amazing possibilities and design your life and your family so you can get there. It all begins with your vision. It took me years to get to this place in my life where I'm incredibly happy, fulfilled, and living with enthusiasm and passion. My vision helped me get here and helps keep me here so I don't stray off-course.

When you don't waste time and energy on negative emotions, you have more time and energy for all the great things in your life. Isn't concentrating on the good things what we should be doing? So take out your journal again. You're going to start outlining your vision for your new happy dual family. Before you start writing, close your eyes and reflect for a little while. Think about your kids. How do you want them to feel about themselves? Do you want them to be confident and happy? What kind of actions will help accomplish that? Will a loving and supportive relationship with both their parents help them develop that strong sense of self? How can you help make that happen? How do you want your kids to feel about your family and you? What actions can you take on a regular basis to help make this happen? Would you like full cooperation between you and your ex in parenting? What does that look like? How will you discuss and resolve parenting and discipline issues? What do you want your relationship with your child to look and feel like? What kind of a connection do you want to have with your children? What steps can you take to make that happen? Go to the "Vision Guide" on the Resources page at www.DualFamily.com/book-resources to find more ideas and questions to ask yourself in creating your vision.

Being very clear in your goals for your dual family will help you make the right decisions going forward. You may even want to share your vision with your ex. Having something in writing you can both refer to from time to time to help you remember what's really important can come in very handy when times get tough.

Working to get along with your ex after a divorce isn't much different from when you're married. You still have to plan, talk through issues together, take a moment to think through a situation, and figure out what to do to achieve your desired outcome. In fact, it's just as important to work on getting along when you're divorced because it's too easy to let the whole darn thing fall apart. After all, you're not married anymore, so you don't *have* to try and make it work. It would be easy to get upset and say, "Forget it! Why am I even bothering with this?" That would be a huge mistake, though, for your kids, your family, and for you.

If you have kids with your ex, whether you like it or not, you'll be highly involved in each other's lives. Do yourself and your kids a favor and work on getting along, even when it's hard and when you have to give in, when it means you have to swallow your pride, or when other people tell you you're wrong. Your vision will help keep you focused in the most difficult situations. Sometimes our egos and emotions sneak up and get the better of us, and we need something to intervene and calm us down. Your vision is this intervention, and you need to be able to pull it out at a moment's notice when you need it. Using it is the easy part. Recognizing when you need to use it can be a little more difficult.

Today, I'm so clear in my desire to keep my family happy, I don't have to revert back to my vision very often. Every now and then though, it comes in very handy. From time to time you, your vision, and the way you've chosen to approach and deal with your dual family will be challenged. Having clarity and faith in your vision for the future will help you overcome those challenges, like when someone tells you you're doing it all wrong.

Here is a good example. Last Thanksgiving was a bit rough for my son. He's a major gamer and had invested more than a year of time, energy, and quite a bit of my money into an online game that he loved to play as much as I would let him. His two step-brothers were using his account to play the game as well. They all had their own characters and had spent months acquiring new characters, battling and moving up levels to further themselves in the game. The problem was, there were three passionate little boys invested in this game, all on the same account. They had to kick each other off the game if they wanted to play because only one person at a time could be on the account. It all came to a head the day before Thanksgiving when each of the boys was complaining about the amount of time they were getting to play the game. All of them felt they weren't getting enough time to play. Evan had just been kicked off the game by one of his step-brothers again, and he was very upset.

This might not seem like a big deal to us adults who are a tad more concerned with how we're going to pay for our little gamer's college education and paying the mortgage on time, but to Evan, this was huge. This game was a big part of his life, and he loved it. So I decided to run interference and called his dad to see what we could do about this. Dad suggested that Evan get his own account, and his step-brothers would keep the existing account. When I relayed this information to Evan, he was devastated. I could see the disappointment in his face. His little shoulders slumped over from their normally confident position, and he started to cry. "That's not fair," he said through his tears. "That's my account. They should get another one." So I came to his aid and suggested to Grant that Evan keep the existing account; after all, it was originally his anyway. Grant didn't think that was going to work. He and Deb, his wife, had been paying for the game for a few months, and her boys didn't want to start the game all over again with a new account either. It was basically two boys against one. So there we were, in a digital quagmire with no agreeable resolution in sight. We had done the time-sharing option by assigning times for the boys to each play, but it just wasn't working. They needed their own accounts, and someone was going to have to boy up and give up their hard work. Who would it be?

As I would recommend you do in this kind of situation, I took a deep breath, referenced my vision for my dual family, and recalled my desire to always keep the peace and only stand my ground on critically important issues. My decision was easy. I knew what I had to do. I sat down with Evan, and told him I was on his side and totally understood that he wanted to keep the account. It was his to begin with, he was nice enough to share it with his step-brothers, and now there were problems. As much as I agreed with his position I had to tell him this was an issue I wasn't willing to force with the family. Evan would have to relinquish his account to his brothers. I explained to Evan why I wasn't willing to go to bat for him on this issue. I'll fight for his health, safety, and emotional well-being all day long, but I won't fight over a game. It just isn't worth the years of effort we've put into creating our happy dual family.

Needless to say, he was extremely disappointed. This

disappointment carried over into Thanksgiving Day when we went over to my parent's house for dinner. Evan was obviously not himself that afternoon, and my family asked why he was so upset. We were all at the table when I explained what happened with the game. A family member was rather annoyed that I didn't do more to stick up for Evan. She said, quite angrily I might add, "You have no backbone! You always give in to Grant. When are you going to stick up for yourself and that kid?" Being very clear in my vision and resolutely committed to it allowed me to confidently respond to her attack. She didn't understand that I was helping Evan in the best way possible by not starting an argument over a stupid thing like a video game. She didn't go through the process, so she didn't understand that to get what you want, you don't take, you give, and you give, even when sometimes it doesn't seem fair. Why? Because it keeps the peace. It keeps the greater family happy, and it keeps us together. It keeps us cooperative and helpful toward each other. Evan understood that. He wasn't happy about it at the time, but he understood.

I did my best to explain why I do the things I do. I explained why I didn't ask for child support and alimony, why I give in on situations like this, and what I actually fight for on Evan's behalf. I still don't think she got it, but that's alright. I don't need to prove why I work to keep my family happy. This isn't a contest or a battle of wills. I go to bat for the really important things rather than the trivial ones. I'm a better person for it, Evan is a happier child for it, and we're a better family for it, too.

The next day, Deb, Grant, all the boys and I went to get our Christmas trees together. Deb had suggested it a couple of weeks earlier, and I was elated for us to be doing this as a dual family for the first time. The boys had a great time running from tree to tree and helping Dad cut them down as Deb and I took pictures and talked. It was great! We wouldn't have been able to do that had I made a stink about the video game and forced Deb's boys to get their own account. It wasn't that I didn't have a backbone. I don't just lie down and take whatever's thrown at me, and I would never suggest you do that, either. The way I see it, I made a trade. I traded the trivial and short-term satisfaction of a video game for the meaningful and long-term happiness of a family. *That* is my backbone. That's what is important to me. And you know what, I took Evan shopping the next day, and he got a new game that he liked even better and didn't have to share with anyone. In two days, he forgot all about the other game. Just think what would have happened if I had made a fuss about the boys having their own account. We'd probably still be fighting over it! It's just not worth it.

No doubt you'll experience issues like this as well. You'll have to learn to choose your battles carefully and refer back to your vision for guidance. It will be of immense help to you. And don't think for one split second that just because you're divorced you won't have family problems anymore. You will! You'll just deal with them a little differently now. Being very clear in your vision will help you get through these little rough patches and enable you to make the best decision for you and your dual family as well and assist you in communicating to your kids why you're handling situations the way you are. They learn valuable lessons in conflict resolution, and you keep your family happy. It's a win-win for everyone!

Creating Your Vision for the Future

At this point you're really progressing on your journey to creating your ideal dual family. That's incredibly exciting! My greatest wish would be that every divorced couple could do what you're doing to keep their family happy and working together. How fantastic would it be to be rid of the bickering and manipulation that so many divorced families live with every day? We'd have happier and healthier parents and kids who have the energy to be the best people they can possibly be.

Speaking of being the best, you've done a great job coming this far. If you've really committed to it, the hardest work is behind you. Make sure you've focused on each part of the process and that you're very comfortable and secure in your vision. If you feel that you still have some unresolved issues, that's fine. Sit with that and work on it more until you're able to work through it. You'll probably still hold bits of anger, frustration, sadness, guilt, or other emotions with you. A little bit it is alright; it's the big chunks that we need to focus on and address here, so do that if you need to.

I've found that writing my feelings in my journal, no matter how silly or irrational they may seem, takes a weight off my shoulders and makes me feel more in control and better overall. Even if I don't resolve anything in my writing, just the act of getting my emotions and thoughts on paper seems to help. You might want to try the same and keep your journal close by for a while and write in it whenever you feel the need. Of course, if you have deep issues that you haven't been able to resolve at this point, you may want to seek the help of a therapist. Having a professional guide you through your recovery after divorce can be immensely helpful. You deserve to be the happiest and healthiest you can be, and divorce can be incredibly difficult. Be sure to reach out for any help you need.

When you're ready and you're clear in your vision, you can move on to the rest of the book, which will help support you in all the work you've done so far and keep your dual family moving in the right direction. Your work isn't quite over yet, so don't get too excited. You'll be working on becoming a better dual family for a long time, but I hope you're seeing that it's worth it. Congratulations on coming this far. Now, let's fine-tune what you've learned by discussing some of the obstacles you'll likely face and how you can keep yourself on track to creating your happy dual family.

Dual Family
STEPS TO SUCCESS

- Use your journal to brainstorm about how you'd like your family to interact after your divorce. Write down all the things you'd like to see happen.

- Create your vision for your happy dual family.

- Go to the "Vision Guide" on the Resources page at www.DualFamily.com/book-resources to get more ideas on creating your vision.

- Review steps one through three in the process, and make sure you've moved through each one as much as possible. Journal about your feelings and thoughts if you have unresolved issues.

- Seek the advice and help of a therapist if you need additional help.

PART 2

Obstacles

"Obstacles don't have to stop you. If you run into a wall, don't turn around and give up. Figure out how to climb it, go through it, or work around it."

—MICHAEL JORDAN

There will be many obstacles on your way to creating your happy dual family, but have no fear. You have me, this book, your vision, and your positive family and friends to help keep you on the straight and narrow to achieve your desired results. The work you've already done in the beginning of the book was the hardest part, at least it was for me. Successfully completing the process in Part 1 will help you better deal with the obstacles and challenges in your dual family that you're likely to face on a regular basis.

Divorce and divorced families have loads of challenges. There are honestly too many to list, so I'm just focusing on what I consider to be the big three. These are issues that occur often and have the potential to hit us hard emotionally and keep us up at night. When you can learn to set the proper limits and guidelines for these issues, your emotions are more controlled, and you'll make better decisions. As a result, life is much simpler and less stressful, and you and your kids will be happier. I'm not into drama and difficulties. I much prefer a positive and uncomplicated life. Being very clear on how I wanted to deal with these key issues kept my life far less complicated, and I was much happier because of it.

What are the big three? You may have encountered them already. Dealing with your ex's new woman/man, money, and scheduling. These are definitely big issues! Each has the potential to wreak havoc on your life and emotions if you don't deal with them correctly. I'll give you some examples and tips on how you can successfully deal with these potentially major drama makers and keep your happy dual family and yourself moving forward in the right direction and drama free.

CHAPTER 4

The New Man or Woman

"Your ability to get along with others will determine your happiness and success as much as any other factor."
—BRIAN TRACY

Let's start with dealing with your ex's new man or woman. This can be a real challenge! No one really wants to see their ex with someone new, and we don't necessarily want this new person around our kids either, right? There's a lot of ego involved here, too. It's easy to let our minds run wild and wonder, is this person better looking than me, nicer, smarter; does he make more money than me; will my kids like her more than me; am I being replaced? Hold on just a minute, though. Don't go crazy. You first need to prep yourself for the reality of this. Your ex will eventually move on to someone else, and that person will be involved in your kids' lives and therefore yours. I know, not an easy reality to face, but you must. So sit with this for a while until you really understand and accept it. It's going to happen. The better prepared you are, the better the outcome.

It happened fairly quickly for me. It must have been only a few weeks after I had moved out that I went to pick up Evan at Grant's house and was introduced to a cute, blonde woman sitting on my couch, in my house, well, the house I moved out of anyway. I was a little shocked to say the least. Grant didn't tell me he had "company." I didn't really have an issue with him dating, but I hadn't expected it so soon. Even though we were getting divorced and I knew this would happen at some point, I wasn't quite ready for it. I felt replaced. I also felt very territorial over my house, my things, and of course, my son. I had 10 years of my belongings in the house. I still had a key to the house and was there at least twice a week. Heck, my dog was still there. I felt like it was still my house. I had bought the darn thing, my name was on the papers, my mail came to that address, and a good number of my cherished belongings were there. Suddenly, there was a new woman, sitting there, in my house. It was a lot to digest.

In person I was very cordial to her and shook her hand while I smiled and said, "Nice to meet you. I'm Evan's mom." That's what came out of my mouth at least. In my head I was saying something more like "Get out of my house, bitch, and back away from my son!" Since this was such an unexpected encounter, it took me a little while to absorb everything and cool down from my bitch stance. First I had to wait for my head to stop spinning.

We had some polite chit-chat, I gathered Evan's things, and we left. As Evan and I drove home I realized this was going to be the new reality for a while. Both Grant and I would be dating and bringing new people into our lives. I couldn't look at every woman as "the bitch in my house." This wasn't looking like a whole lot of fun to me. When you split up or divorce, you logically know that encountering a new partner with your ex is inevitable, but you have absolutely no idea what that's going to look and feel like until it happens. Having it sprung on you unexpectedly doesn't make it any easier. So I appealed to my practical side to search for the best way to deal with this, and after some time noodling on it for a bit, and maybe a few more realizations of "Shit, I can't believe that just happened!" I came up with the answer. Ground rules! Yep, that was it, ground rules! Grant and I needed to talk and work out some ground rules around the dating scene.

When Grant and I separated, we agreed and made a pledge to each other that no matter who else came into our lives or whatever happened, we would always put our family unit first. Just because you're divorced doesn't mean you're not a family anymore. You're just a different kind of family. For us, our family unit of three had to come first.

When you constructed your vision for your dual family and what you wanted it to look and feel like, I suggested you share that with your ex to make sure you're both on the same page. If you haven't done that, now might be a good time to revisit your goals and vision and have your ex over for dinner or meet for coffee or whatever is comfortable for you so you can discuss it. If you didn't anticipate having a section in your vision for how to deal with the new significant other in your ex's life, take some time and add that in now. Think about how you'd like that person to interact with you and with your kids. Do you want to have just a civil relationship with not a lot of interaction with that person or a good relationship where you can talk comfortably and have more of a partnership? Would you like to eventually have a friendship with that person or deal with them as little as possible? Do you want that person to be another parent to your kids or be just a friend? Think about what you'd truly like to have in the most ideal sense. Create the best-case scenario for you and your dual family. Building a great relationship with your ex's new partner is completely possible, but it will take effort, time, some swallowing of pride, shelving your ego and maybe a few tears, too.

Later that night I called Grant and basically gave him the ol' "What the hell? Why didn't you tell me you had someone over?" He responded with "Did that bother you?" "Well, yes," I said. "I would have appreciated a little notice." This led to a discussion of the situation in more detail, and we came up with a few hard and fast rules we promised each other we would abide by. We agreed that neither one of us would move away, even if we fell madly in love with someone from out of the area. Our family was here, and our family was primary, so we agreed to stay here. We also agreed to let each other know if we had someone over so we weren't surprised. We wanted to meet that person if a true and meaningful relationship started, especially if they were around our son a lot. Anyone we brought into our lives had to be great with Evan and understand that he comes first, and they had to be comfortable with us getting along as a family. At that point we were nowhere near where we are now with getting along but we didn't hate each other, and that was enough to make some of the new people in our lives very uncomfortable and insecure.

Not everyone is secure enough to be comfortable with you having a good relationship with your ex. You need to be able to know early on who those people are and get rid of them fast. They aren't likely to change, and their negative energy could ruin your chances of having a happy dual family. I know that's much easier said than done. Before you start to get serious with someone, tell them straight up: "I have a good relationship with my ex, and I'm working on making it even better for our family. How do you feel about that?" Reassure them that there is nothing romantic between you and your ex, but that you want a healthy and happy family life, and that includes getting along well with your ex. Present a few scenarios of how you interact with your ex to your potential new partner and see what he/she says. For instance, ask what they would think if you all went to the movies together, or how they would feel if you talk on the phone with your ex several times a week about your children and family issues. These conversations will give you big clues as to how your potential new partner is going to react to your dual family situation. If you think your new flame isn't going to be on board, say goodbye, and fast! Hard to do, yes, but it would be even harder for you to deal with a nasty, jealous partner who's trying to undermine your dual family. Believe me, there's plenty of those people out there. Emotionally healthy, secure, and mature people will likely be just fine with this. Insecure, needy, emotionally unhealthy people probably won't. Ask yourself, which would you prefer in your life and in your child's life?

For the most part, my ex and I had really good luck with the people we dated. Just about everyone was understanding and supportive of our family situation. I dated one guy who waffled a bit back and forth with his support of our dual family. He blew up when I suggested we all go on vacation together for my son's birthday. That relationship didn't last too long. Grant dated one winner, who to this day, still holds a special place in our family history for being the worst person in our lives, ever! We called her "Kelly, the Bitch." The name has been changed to protect the guilty, but you get the idea.

You have to be very careful about the people you allow into your dual family. The right person can help unite the family together and enrich the lives of you and your children, and the wrong person can break you and your kids down and tear your family apart. We began to experience the latter with Kelly the Bitch, and boy was she ever!

Grant and Kelly had been seeing each other for a few months, and she refused to meet me. Every time Grant asked her to meet me, she came up with some excuse or insisted she "just wasn't ready yet." Ready for what? If you're dating someone who is so insecure they can't bring themselves to meet your ex, get rid of them. This is a huge red flag! That type of insecurity belongs nowhere around you or your kids. You and they deserve much better.

When Kelly eventually moved into the house with Grant and Evan, I put my foot down. Now she was living with my child. That meant she would have a daily influence on him, and I needed to meet her. I was surprised Grant had let it go this far. I reminded him about the ground rules we had agreed to and promised each other we'd follow. So the next time I came over to the house, there she was, waiting with a smile. She was very friendly and seemed quite pleasant. I sat down so the three of us could all talk for a while. After about 10 minutes of polite chit-chat, some smiles and a few laughs, Evan and I left. I thought it all went pretty well. I got a call from Grant later on. Apparently she didn't feel the same.

Kelly complained to Grant that I had mentioned he and I a few too many times in conversation, and she felt that I was over-asserting myself with her, staking my claim if you will, with him and the family. I was floored! I told Grant that was absolutely not my intention. He laughed and kind of shrugged it off and said, "I know, I think she's just a little intimidated by you." Once again, if the person you're dating is intimidated by your ex, drop 'em, and find someone else! It will only lead to problems down the road as it did with us.

Kelly's insecurity caused her to attempt to exert more control over our family. She tried to force Evan to eat certain foods and punished him if he didn't. She set some rules in the house that shut out Evan's interaction with his dad. Evan wasn't allowed to open the master bedroom door if it was closed, even if he really needed something. Keep in mind, he was only about 4 years old at this time, so this could have been a major safety issue for Evan. She didn't like it when Evan and Grant spent alone time together. She always wanted to be a part of it. And she put his physical safety at risk by not buckling him into his car seat time and time again. She didn't cherish him and didn't respect the relationship that Grant, Evan, and I had as a family. It wasn't looking good, and Evan was starting to act out. He had never had behavioral problems before. He had always been such a well-behaved little boy, so when he started hitting, crying, and being difficult, seemingly for no real reason, I knew something was very wrong.

I always tried to call Evan on my way into work in the mornings. I liked starting my day by saying hello and telling him I loved him. If I couldn't be with him when he was at his dad's, talking to him every morning I was away was the next best thing. I called one morning to say hi to my baby, and he picked up the phone. "Good morning, angel, how are you?" I asked. "Hi mommy. I'm hungry." I thought that a little odd since it was about 8 am already, and he probably should have had breakfast by now, but maybe they all slept a little late. I said, "That's OK, baby; just go tell Daddy you want breakfast, and he'll make it for you." In his cutest little 4-year-old voice, he replied with "I can't." Suddenly, I was a little more alert and tuned in very closely to his words. "What do you mean you can't?" I asked, waiting anxiously for his reply. "I'm not allowed to go into daddy's room if the door is closed, or I'll get in trouble," he said.

You can imagine how I felt when I heard that. I knew who was behind this, and I certainly was not going to stand for it. No one is going to treat my child like that. I said, "No you won't, sweetie, I promise. You hold onto the phone, and knock on the door, and you tell daddy I want to speak with him." On the verge of tears at this point, Evan said, "But I'll get in trouble." She obviously had quite a bit of control and power in that house, and that scared me. It scared my son, too. Evan got his breakfast that morning, but that situation made me realize just how dangerous it can be to let the wrong person into our lives.

Things got a little worse over the next couple of months. I was asked not to call in the mornings, and she didn't want me picking up Evan at the house either. I was slowly being squeezed out of my family's life. It got so bad that I actually thought about suing

Grant for full custody, and I even contacted a couple of attorneys. That idea had never entered my mind before Kelly came into our lives. I remember standing on my front porch with Grant one night after he had dropped off Evan. I was crying and reciting what we had promised each other years before, that we would never let anyone come between our family, but she was! I was terrified I was going to lose my family to this hideous woman, and worse than that, my baby boy was being harmed by her. I told him that if things didn't change, I would be suing him for full custody. No one liked this woman. Even his family didn't like her, and I couldn't imagine spending the rest of my life dealing with Kelly the Bitch! That wasn't part of our plan.

Thankfully, within a month or so, she was gone, and we were all so much happier as life got back to normal, and we could be free with our communication with each other and spending time together again. Evan seemed instantly happier, and his behavioral problems went away within a couple of weeks. I had my happy, confident, loving and affectionate baby back. It was a good lesson in what *not* to do. It drove home to me, and I think Grant, too, that our family has to come first; when we stray from that, everything is more difficult.

I was thrilled when about a year later, Grant introduced me to Deb. She was attractive, nice, intelligent, had two boys of her own, and we got along great! She wasn't threatened or intimidated by me, and she adored Evan. I jokingly told Grant that if he didn't marry her, I'd kill him! To this day we still get along great, have an open line of communication, and work together as two moms in a dual family.

I have to admit, the first time Evan called Deb "Mom," I was a little shocked, and even a little hurt and offended. But when I took my ego out of it and thought about it, it was true, she was a mom to him, and thank goodness! If I can't be with him all the time, isn't it better to have another mom there who will take care of him like he's her own? I never have to worry about Evan when he's on vacation with her or if he gets hurt at their house or if something happens to him at school and they can't reach me. Deb is always there to help and take care of him. They have a wonderful relationship, and it brings me so much comfort when I'm away from him. She's a great spouse to Grant, a wonderful step-mom to my child, and a good friend to me. It doesn't get much better than that!

You may be wondering if I felt at all threatened by her and her relationship with Evan. I can honestly say I never did. This is largely credited to the very close and deep relationship I've developed over the years with Evan. No matter who else comes into Evan's life, I know no one will ever be able to break our bond. It's something I worked to reinforce for years and continue to build on regularly today, and we are solid because of it. To her credit, too, she never tried to show me up, buy Evan's affections, or go out of her way to do crazy things for him in an attempt to win his favor. But even if she took him to his favorite restaurant every week and bought him a new toy whenever he wanted, I couldn't really do much about that. We can't control other people's behavior. We can only control our own. I'm very secure in my relationship with my son, he knows that I love him more than anyone else in the world possibly could, and I work on strengthening our relationship daily.

If you feel that another man or woman may jeopardize your relationship with your child, then you might want to work on your relationship with your child to make sure that you are more comfortable and secure in that relationship. If you become jealous or controlling, your behavior toward your ex, their new partner, and even your child may change, and that could affect how your dual family interacts.

We'll be working on this more a little later in the book, but right now, grab your journal again, and jot down what you'd like to improve about your relationship with your kids. What would you like to do more of and less of? What type of activities do you like to do together? How can you carve out more time to spend together doing meaningful things, not just being in the house together? The great thing is, you can start to improve your relationship with your kids right now! Give your kids a call and just tell them you love and miss them. When they come home, eat dinner together, without the TV or electronics, then take a walk and just talk. It might not be easy at first, but the conversations will start happening. Something Evan and I do almost every night together is cuddle up before we go to sleep and spend at least 10 or so minutes just talking about whatever. We get real close to each other, and talk, laugh, and be silly. It's a great way to end the day. When you have a close and meaningful relationship with your kids, no one and nothing can come between that. Not money, not the latest video game, not taking them on the coolest vacation ever, nothing! You have to work at it, it's not a one-time thing, and you can't buy your way into it because it has nothing to do with money. You have to actively participate and do it every day. I promise you the rewards are well worth it. If your ex happens to date someone a little less than desirable from time to time, you'll at least be secure in knowing that your relationship with your kids is solid. And that is a great feeling!

I want to mention one last thing about bringing a new person into your family and the lives of your children. Not only do you and your ex have to be careful about the type of person you bring into the fold, but you have to be very careful in how you handle your relationship with new people and what they convey to your kids. This is critical. Remember, your kids are watching and learning from you with every step you take. Are you setting a good example by dating and getting to know a good person who's genuinely interested in you and your kids and is considerate and respectful of your family and how he or she treats you and treats your kids? Or are you bringing home a new person every week who barely knows the names of your children, let alone has much of an interest in them or the values of your family? What your kids see you do and how they experience your actions may affect how they perceive men, women and relationships in their own lives. Their view of relationships, how they treat others, and how they want to be treated themselves will be influenced by what they see and experience you do.

Being divorced can sometimes be lonely, and that's OK—it's expected. If your ex is dating a fantastic person and you're not dating anyone, don't succumb to the loneliness and be with the wrong kind of person or be in the wrong relationship just because it's convenient or easy. Remember the easy vs. hard decisions we talked about earlier? Don't go the easy route for immediate gratification that you know is only going to screw you in the long run. Do your kids and yourself a favor and set the right example for them. You're their greatest teacher, and your lessons should always show them the best possible path to follow. Showing up with a new date every week or moving in with your new boyfriend after only two months probably isn't it.

Dual Family
STEPS TO SUCCESS

▸ Get your journal and prepare yourself for the reality of your ex dating. How do you feel about that? How will you deal with it when it happens? Is this something you can talk to your ex about and set some parameters around?

▸ What kind of a relationship would you like to have with your ex's new partner? Would you prefer to have a friendly relationship or not have to interact much? Think about how that will look on a day-to-day basis.

▸ Once you're comfortable with your decision, incorporate it into your vision.

▸ We can always work on building a great relationship with our kids. What can you do to improve your relationship with your kids? How can you build an even closer bond than you have now? Write down some ideas of things you can do on a regular basis to bring you and your kids closer.

Chapter 5

Money, Money, Money

"The safest way to double your money is to
fold it over and put it in your pocket."
—Kin Hubbard

Ah, money! We must have it. It's what makes our modern world
go around, and it's what brings some exes to the ground.
Like many issues in a divorce, money is a very emotional matter.
If you both worked while married, it's scary to know that you
won't have that second income. If you weren't working outside
the home in the marriage, you might have to look for a job. That
can be pretty scary, too. Divorcing may also derail your plans for
retirement, your savings plan, the college fund for your kids, that
vacation you love to take every year, and other financial goals.
In a divorce, however, it is what we must deal with and move
forward as best we can without destroying the other person.

Not long ago, I met a woman who was recently divorced. She
explained to me that she *had to* get a lawyer to tell her what she
deserved out of the relationship, and she wanted every penny that
was owed to her. She kept saying that he owed her and she didn't
care what it did to him. Her stance was very confrontational. She

didn't care what her ex was left with. She wanted everything she felt was due to her regardless of how it affected him or her children. She was in deserving mode, not preserving mode.

This is a very adversarial stance. "You owe me!" or "I deserve this!" is likely to instantly create tension and animosity. Once you've done that and fought about the money and caused your ex financial hardship, you can just about kiss your happy dual family goodbye. It's more difficult for your ex to want to form a friendship with you or even a cooperative family relationship after that's happened. I'm not saying it can't happen, but it makes it much harder.

I know, you might be thinking, Shouldn't I have what's rightfully mine? Yes, absolutely you are entitled to a portion of the estate created in your marriage. The laws around this change from state to state, so be sure you look into what the law is in your state. To research online, try a legal resource site like Nolo.com, or speak with your mediator about it. If you don't have a mediator, you can find one at www.Mediate.com or www.DivorceMediators. com. You can also find quite a bit of information on Nolo's divorce site, www.DivorceNet.com, where property division by state is discussed. On the home page for DivorceNet, go to the "Resources by State" section on the right-hand side and click on your state.

Although you should receive your fair share of the assets, the way you go about getting it and your attitude around it makes all the difference. Get out of the deserving, selfish, "I'm gonna take that witch for everything she's got" mode, and think more in terms of what you need to do to preserve your happy dual family. I know it's easy to want to "get back" at your ex and fight to take a ton of his or her money, but we're doing things a little differently, right? You aren't going to be like everyone else. You're above that kind of behavior.

When you're feeling contentious and adversarial, or even fearful around the issue of money, take a deep breath, step back, and get out of the heat of the moment. Take a walk, write your feelings and thoughts in your journal, talk with a positive friend, and revisit your goals for your dual family. Ask yourself, "Is the way I'm handling this situation going to help me reach my goal of a happy dual family and a good relationship with my ex, now and in the long run?" It's a tough question because right about now, fighting and taking your ex for everything they've got might sound a whole lot more satisfying than trying to get along. Fight those negative and unproductive urges though. Stay positive and strong. Think cooperatively and look at options that will work well for you and for your ex instead of just at what you want or what you think you can get.

When Grant and I separated, we used a mediator instead of lawyers. This diffused the tension of the situation immediately because we weren't opposing each other in court, which is a very confrontational place to begin with. We were working together to achieve a mutual decision. Not only did we feel much more cooperative toward each other, but we saved a ton of money. The mediator was less than $1,000 compared to several thousand for an attorney. We sat down calmly and went through all our assets and split them as evenly as we could. We liquidated our available cash and split that as well. Our mediator helped us to address issues like child care, savings, and paying for college, medical and dental care, and other necessities. When all was said and done, we walked away from our marriage with our assets fairly shared between us. I didn't ask for alimony or child support, and in lieu of this my ex agreed to pay for child care until our son was in first grade. This gave me enough time to get back on my feet and save some money. Short-term trade-offs like this can work very well to get both parties what they want in a divorce without one person feeling like they're locked into a lifetime commitment they really aren't happy with. Consider something like this if you're having trouble reaching an agreement on an issue.

I didn't ask for a portion of his retirement or pension either, although I could have. To me that was just grasping for something else to dig into him with, and it seemed silly. I wanted to be able to stand on my own two feet and not have him reminded every time he saw me that he'd still be paying me 30 years from now. We split our current assets in a way we felt was fair and made both of us comfortable for the most part. I'm sure he would have been happier keeping more, and I certainly would have liked to have kept more, too. We both gave up some things, but in the end, it worked, and we were both OK with it. We were able to move on in a civilized manner toward each other because we dealt with this contentious issue with calm and level heads, about as much as you can in a divorce anyway.

When I tell people (especially men) that I didn't fight my ex for child support or alimony, their jaws usually hit the floor. Men say they wished they had divorced me instead of their money-grubbing ex-wife. "Why in the world would you do that?" is generally the response. Because that wasn't the way I wanted to end my marriage and start a new life. Fighting isn't fun. It isn't productive, and it doesn't feel good. We both benefitted financially from each other in the marriage in many different ways, and when it was time to separate, it only seemed fair that we split everything 50/50 and leave it pretty much at that.

When in doubt about how to handle a conversation or issue with money or anything else, revert back to your vision for your happy dual family. Do you want to fight, or do you want to get along? Fighting over money may cause deep wounds to go even deeper and prevent you from becoming a happy dual family. Look at your vision and throw consistently fighting over money into the plan. You can spend years bickering over late child support payments, not to mention the ridiculous attorney fees that it will cost you, if you take your ex to court over support payments that are never made. Arguing over who's going to buy new shoes for school, who pays for the latest dental appointment, and who'll shell out the cash for the new soccer uniform isn't fun. How does your vision look now? It can't possibly look peaceful and sane.

I'm not saying don't ask for child support or alimony. Just because I felt that was the right decision for me doesn't mean it's the right approach for you. The point is to go about the money issue in a more level-headed and cooperative way. Don't try to bleed your ex dry; instead divide things as evenly and as calmly as possible so you both are happy and feel fairly treated. This is what will help create harmony. Don't get discouraged if this takes a little while, and don't be afraid to ask for help. A counselor or mediator can shed a lot of light on the situation and help bring you both toward more common ground. Both of you will need to give in on different things, and one of you may need to give where you really don't want to, just to put an end to the whole thing. Whatever decisions you make, be sure you'll be able to live permanently with them.

I made an earlier reference to living small in Chapter 2, and I think it's worth mentioning again. What exactly is living small? It's being happy with what you have, even if it isn't ideal, and not trying to show up your ex or anyone else by buying things you really can't afford just to try and make yourself look good for everyone else. Now is not the time to live big, go on an expensive vacation, or buy things you can't afford that will put you into debt for years just so you can try to show everyone how well adjusted you are and how great you're doing. Cars, clothes, jewelry, houses, and other things are not what you should be focusing on now. If you have to move, try renting a small house and see what it's like to be physically near your kids. You might find you actually like it, and they might, too! It may even help you all get along better, making you feel more secure and happier as a family. If you're fortunate enough to get a large settlement from your divorce, don't go crazy and buy a sports car. Instead, save your money, invest it, pay off any debt you have, and start your new life on a solid financial footing. It's incredibly satisfying to be a divorced parent on your own for the first time and have strong finances with money in the bank, no debt and a solid savings plan. Now *that* is empowering and will make you feel great!

Living small also means you don't have to keep up with the Joneses and do what everyone else does. Spend some time talking with your kids, taking walks or bike rides together, or playing a board game instead of shopping and going out to eat. None of these things cost money, yet they give you the richness of a loving and close family that money can't possibly buy. Get rid of your house cleaner and spend an afternoon with your kids tidying up the house. It's a good lesson in responsibility for them, helps you out, and saves money at the same time.

Living small and saving your money allows you to have money in the bank instead of debt on your credit cards. Money in the bank feels so much better! When you don't have to worry about how you're going to pay the bills, buy that new pair of shoes for school, or pay for braces, your heart, mind and emotions are open to devote to your children and creating a loving and close family. And remember, it isn't how much you make or, in the case of divorce, take, but how much you keep that counts. Try living small and spending even smaller. Allow your savings account to grow and see how wonderful and empowering that feels. You'll be making wise decisions for your finances and teaching your kids good financial habits as well.

Unless you're really great with your money, I would suggest consulting a financial professional or even a good book about money, saving, and investing. One I particularly like and is written in very plain language is Dave Ramsey's *Total Money Makeover*. He provides some great tips on saving and investing, what's important to spend your money on, and how to save day to day. It's an unintimidating read and very helpful.

Be smart when you divide your assets. If you own a home, cars, or have credit cards together, or anything else with a payment that you financed as a couple, you must treat these things with extra care to ensure your liability is removed. For instance, if you own a home together and your ex is keeping the house, make sure the loan is refinanced, if there is one, and your ex takes out a new loan solely in their name so your name is no longer on the loan documents. Taking your name off the deed or title isn't enough. You're still liable for the mortgage or loan as long as your name is on it. It doesn't matter what you agreed to in your divorce settlement or if your ex swears up and down that he will make the full payment on time and keep it current. You never know what may happen down the road. If your ex loses their job and can't make the payment, your credit will suffer because your name is still on the loan. Make sure your ex refinances the house and the new loan papers are drawn without your name on them. During the escrow process for the refinance you can sign the papers to take your name off the deed, and not before. It's the same thing if you own a car and have a loan on it together. If your ex keeps the car and stops making the payments on it and your name is on the loan, guess who the lender is coming after? Whose credit score is going to drop because of the non-payments? Be fair in splitting up your assets, but be smart, too.

Consult a financial advisor or tax consultant if there are issues you don't know how to deal with. This way, you'll be doing the right things the right way, and there will be far fewer reasons for you and your ex to fight over money down the road. Be smart, do your homework, and think preserve, not deserve. Ah, I can sense the happy dual family growing already!

Dual Family
STEPS TO SUCCESS

- ▸ Try to handle the financial aspects of your split cooperatively and fairly. Stay away from deserving mode and work toward preserving.

- ▸ Make sure you know the property division laws in your state. Consult your mediator or go to www.DivorceNet.com. To find a mediator, try www.Mediate.com or www.DivorceMediators.com.

- ▸ Consider short-term trade-offs for those issues you're having a hard time agreeing on.

- ▸ Focus on living small, and start building your financial security.

- ▸ Be smart about dividing your assets, especially when you have loans or credit cards in both your names. Consult a financial professional for advice if you need to.

Chapter 6

The Art of Scheduling

"There cannot be a crisis today;
my schedule is already full."
—Henry Kissinger

This used to be our biggest and most constant challenge and still throws us for a loop every now and then. There seems to always be a scheduling crisis around the corner, until you learn how to deal with it. There are steps you can take to make life easier for you, your children, and your ex if you hone in on the problem areas and look for solutions.

When you first get divorced, the task of arranging and scheduling time with your kids is a little daunting and very foreign. You may have been used to making your children breakfast every morning, having dinner with them every night, and helping them with their homework every evening, but now you have to set a schedule to see them for a fraction of the time you used to have with them. Not being able to see or speak with your child whenever you want is odd to say the least. With these kinds of constraints around the time you and your children spend together, it's no wonder parents get a little defensive about their allotted time with their kids and sticking to the schedule. Requesting that the kids be back on time regularly is reasonable, but nasty quarrels about your ex being 10 minutes late to drop off the kids has the potential to cause a major rift. I know it's hard to not take those lost minutes personally. You only get so much time with your kids, so you want to take advantage of every second you can possibly have with them, which is understandable.

Try not to be defensive about every minute of "your" time with the kids, though. More critical than the amount of time you spend with your children is the *quality* of time you spend with them. I would rather have one or two really high-quality days with Evan, where we're engaged with each other and truly spending the time bonding and having fun, than five days of just hanging around the house. Time for time's sake isn't all that important; it's what you do with that time that counts.

During the mediation and negotiation process of divorce, or if you're working with an attorney, you likely will deal with setting a schedule with your kids. We originally set a defined schedule that worked fine for a while, but when we became a happy dual family we relaxed and began setting our schedule week by week. This was so much better for me because my work schedule changes frequently. It also allowed my ex to make changes that fit best with his schedule, and Evan still got enough time with both of us. Your schedule may change from its original design as well. Regardless of whether you have a set schedule or one that changes regularly, keeping a few key best practices in mind will help make scheduling easier on you, your kids, your ex, and your dual family.

The Art of Scheduling

Here are a few scheduling pointers:

- *Make it as easy and simple as possible.* Too much structure and too many rules are likely to end up being difficult for you, your ex, and especially your kids.
- *Don't plan out too far in advance—especially* if one of you has a job where your work schedule is apt to change at the last minute. Try planning just one week at a time, aside from holidays and vacations.
- *Take your ex's schedule into account.* If he or she works odd hours and has a schedule that's likely to change frequently, try to roll with it as much as you can.
- *Don't punish your ex for being late to drop the kids off or early to pick them up.* Remember, when you're flexible with your ex, your ex is more likely to be flexible with you.
- *Try a fluid schedule instead of a set schedule every week.* Many couples choose to do the three days on and three days off with every other weekend schedule. This can work great and can create a sense of consistency and order, but it doesn't allow for much variation if you have a job that requires you to be more flexible with your time. We organize our schedule week by week, depending on our individual needs that particular week.
- *Take a cue from your kids.* If your kids desperately miss their mom or dad, let them go back early. Their needs and desires change; they're kids after all, so be flexible and give them what they need, even if it's not what you'd prefer. They'll thank you for it.
- *When you're ready, consider spending special days together as a dual family so no one is left out and the kids don't feel pulled*

in too many directions. Your children's birthdays are a great place to start. Having one family party not only saves money, but it makes the kids feel great when everyone is together.

- *Involve your kids in the planning of their schedule.* If your kids are past the age of 5 or 6, sit down and ask them where they'd like to spend their time. Go over the schedule you and your ex have prepared for that week. Ask them if it sounds good to them or if they'd like something different. As Evan has gotten older, we've let him choose how much time he'd like to spend at each house. He gets his needs met, and because he helped in the planning, he feels like he has some control over his life, which makes him a happier child.

- *Make plans for the holidays and vacations well in advance and discuss with your ex.* We had a vacation snafu this year for the first time. It wasn't good and caused some conflict. We're much more careful now to notify everyone as soon as we want to make plans for a getaway. Getting everyone in agreement early on avoids issues as these important dates draw near.

- *Look for signs of stress in your kids.* Every child is different. Packing up and going back and forth between houses can be very stressful to some kids. Imagine how you'd feel if you were in a different place every couple of days. If your child is exhibiting signs of stress, not sleeping, unusually acting out or crying, hitting or throwing tantrums, or having problems in school, take a few calm minutes and have a little chat with them. I've found that bedtime is a great time for this. You both are relaxed, and there's nothing else to focus on except each other. Ask them how they're feeling, how they feel about being at mom's house and at dad's house and what their needs are. You can learn a lot from just a few minutes of open communication. Be sure to truly listen and then respond appropriately to your child's needs. This isn't a contest to see who your child wants to spend more time with. Take your emotions and ego out of this and listen to what your child is saying.

- *Set a routine for when your kids are home so they have some security knowing what to expect when they're with you.* Plan some special time with your kids as often as you can. If possible, it's ideal to have some continuity with schedules and routines at both houses. Not everything will be the same, of course, but maybe you and your ex can start by agreeing on a mutual bedtime.

- *Make it a rule that you both can call the kids when they're away from you.* You may need to institute a timeframe, say, not before 7 am and no later than 8 pm, but knowing that you can talk with your kids every day when they're away is a huge comfort and makes being away from them so much easier. I talk with Evan almost every day he's with his dad and sometimes he calls me just to say hi. It's good and healthy for everyone to have open communication and for the kids to be able to speak with a parent when they want or need to.

- *Whenever possible, try not to rush when picking up and dropping off your kids.* This can create additional stress for everyone. You never want to leave your kids in a frenzied rush or drop them off without taking a brief moment to give them a warm hug and kiss and tell them how much you love them. A pleasant transition from house to house is such a great way to begin and end your time together.

You have the ability to make scheduling as difficult or as easy as possible. I vote for easy! The path of least resistance is a common thread in this book. If you're well prepared, involve your kids in the planning, and don't get mad at your ex for being early or late with the kids, then you're on your way to successful scheduling that will support the needs of your children and give you the quality time you need with them. For more scheduling tips, go to www.DualFamily.com and download additional information from the Resources page.

One last word on scheduling, I know it can seem like the world ends when you don't have your kids with you, especially in the beginning. To create happiness out of divorce you have to look at the positive side of everything. Learn to create good things out of the time you aren't with your kids. You can use it for personal enrichment time, working to make more money, improving your health by exercising, going back to school, just about anything. I was able to enjoy some hobbies that I never would have had time for if Evan had been with me. Granted, I would have loved to have been with him every day, but the reality was that wasn't going to happen, so I had to make the best of it. Through my hobbies I was able to meet wonderful people and do things that made me happy and enriched my life. I never would have had time to write this book if Evan had been with me every day.

Take a moment, grab your journal, and make a list of some of the things you'd like to do when your kids aren't with you. Take action right now and choose one of those things to do the next day you don't have your kids. Keep doing this until you find things you love to do and make you happy. Soon the time away from your kids won't be so difficult, and you'll be growing and enriching your life in positive ways.

Dual Family
STEPS TO SUCCESS

▸ Make scheduling easy!

▸ Try not to be defensive about every moment of *your* time.

▸ Go for high-quality time with your kids, not just quantity.

▸ Keep this chapter's scheduling pointers in mind when setting your schedule.

▸ Go to www.DualFamily.com/book-resources for additional resources on scheduling.

▸ Get your journal and make a list of the things you can do with the time your kids aren't with you. Take action and commit to doing one of those things the next time your kids are with your ex.

PART 3

Secrets
of a Happy
Dual Family

"Welcome to our big old happy
dysfunctional family. You are now in,
and whether you like it or not,
you can never get out."

—HAYLEY WILLIAMS

By this point in your quest to create a happy dual family, you're hopefully at a fairly solid place in your relationship with your ex. Just remember, this relationship is fluid. Sometimes it's going to work really well, and you're going to think "Wow, this is great that we're all getting along so well. This dual family stuff really works!" Other times you'll be more likely to curse me while you lament the lameness of your ex's behavior. It's not always going to be sunshine and roses for you and your dual family. Sometimes it's going to stink, and sometimes it's going to be spectacular. I'm hoping it's more of the latter for you.

Every day there are things you can do to help improve the quality of your dual family, your relationship with your kids, and your own happiness. This is a work-in-progress on all fronts, and just like any other relationship you have to work on it if you want it to improve. It will certainly pay off in the end.

I'm often asked how we're able to keep our dual family so consistently happy, even after all these years. Well, there are definitely a few secrets I've learned along the way. They're all common sense, but it's great to have a reminder because in the often stressful world of divorce, we tend to forsake what's common sense for the emotions of the moment. Stepping back, taking a deep breath, analyzing a situation, then dealing with it in a more level-headed and cooperative manner is what will keep you and your dual family happy and healthy for years to come. These secrets can help you do just that. Don't just read them here, then forget about them. Remind yourself of them regularly. To help you keep them front of mind, download the cheat sheet "Secrets of a Happy Dual Family" at www.DualFamily.com/book-resources.

Just as it was with the process you went through in Part 1, you're going to have to do the work here. A better, happier, more communicative divorced family isn't going to happen on its own. A successful dual family requires consistency, but the good thing is, the more you practice these secrets, the easier they become. That's why you need your cheat sheet to help remind you every day so you don't veer off course. Before you know it, you'll be working these secrets like a pro and not even realize you're doing it. Since making a happy dual family is largely about you, let's start with the secrets that focus on you.

CHAPTER 7

SECRET #1: You Are in Control of You and Only You

"To handle yourself, use your head.
To handle others, use your heart."

—ELEANOR ROOSEVELT

While these words in Secret #1 may sound very logical, in the heat of an ex-marital battle dealing with the kids, schedules, money issues, and all the other challenges divorced life brings, it's easy to lose sight of this and blame your ex for everything that isn't perfect in your life. But the truth is, we can only control our own thoughts, actions, and reactions—nothing more. We can't even control our kids. As much as we sometimes would like to, the best we can do is lead them with good examples, love them, instill in them good ethics and values, and hope they do the right thing when the time comes and we're not there.

It's really the same thing with your dual family. The best you can do is make sure you're in the right frame of mind to create a happy dual family, then do what you can to develop that happiness. Your ex may or may not be on board with your dual family plan. Hopefully, she is. If you've already discussed your vision with your ex, then he has a good idea of what you want to do and hopefully is at least somewhat on board. Even if your ex is not, you can still approach him and your dual family with a spirit of cooperation, and at the very least, your kids will be getting a great example from you. I know it's tough when your ex is being a jerk, manipulating your kids, and not telling the truth seemingly about anything, but you can't control any of that. You can only set the right example, try your best to be the bigger person, and show your ex the way to a happy dual family. Whether or not they choose to follow is up to them.

I have to be honest: This may or may not work for your ex. She may never come around to your vision of being a happy dual family and might always act like a raving lunatic. So what do you do when your ex isn't cooperating and isn't agreeing with your approach with your kids? What do you do when your ex seems to be fighting you on every front and you can't seem to reach common ground? Let's take a look at some examples.

I met Julie at a seminar we both attended about unleashing your talents and passions. We got to chatting about what each of us is passionate about, and I brought up this book. This happens a lot; she instantly perked up and said, "I'm divorced and my ex and I have such a hard time getting along. Can you help?" She went on to tell me that she desperately wants to have a happy family, but her ex, Paul, is very difficult to get along with. He's resentful that she remarried before he did and that she has the kids most of the time. He's also a controller and makes a major fuss any time something happens with the kids that he doesn't like. They can't seem to get on the same page with just about anything. They can't even agree on a standard bedtime at each house. The kids are at Julie's house during the week for school, where they go to bed by about 9 pm every night so they get a full night's sleep. They get up about 6:30 am for school. But when they go to their dad's house on the weekends, they stay up past midnight and sleep in until whenever they wake up. There's no set bedtime schedule at Paul's.

That might not sound like a big deal, but keep in mind these kids are in elementary school and it can be hard for kids that age to adjust to that wide a variance in schedules. Julie said she discussed this issue with her ex a couple of times to no avail. After years of back and forth on this subject, the boys still go to bed early at her house and late at their dad's. There's absolutely nothing she can do about it, so she has resigned herself to that reality. Although she would prefer for the boys to have the same bedtime at each house, she knows no amount of complaining, arguing, or bringing the issue back up from time to time is going to change it. She understands she's only in control of her actions, so she tries not to worry about what Paul does. She asked if I had any suggestions for dealing with her ex on this subject. Although she was looking for a miracle suggestion that would instantly change everything for the better, I had to tell her I think she's handling it the right way. We can't be control freaks about what happens at our ex's when our kids are there, and if your ex is a little on the vindictive side, he may even push your buttons on purpose and not relent on an issue just because he knows it's important to you. Julie found ways to compensate for the change in schedule when the boys were at her house. She held firm to her weekday night and morning routines so the boys knew what to expect, and when they returned on Sunday afternoons, she made sure they had lots of exercise and were ready for an earlier bedtime. That's about as much as she can do because that's what she can control. Doing that instead of worrying about it and arguing incessantly with her ex gives her some peace of mind, which means she has more energy to focus on making her time with her boys fun and enjoyable.

Even an experienced happy dual family like mine has challenges from time to time. When challenges come our way, I reference my vision and these secrets so I'm better able to keep myself and my family on track. For example, I was over at my ex's house the other night having dinner with the family. Evan mentioned to me that he hadn't finished his homework yet because he needed his dad's help with it. It was getting a little late, about 7 pm, and I was becoming concerned that he might not be able to finish his work for school. After dinner the kids watched a movie, and Grant, Deb and I were chatting in the other room. When 8 pm rolled around, Evan still hadn't finished his homework. I was nervous at this point, but my ex is very laid back. I really had to bite my tongue to keep from saying something about Evan needing to get the homework done. This was his house, and we were on his schedule, which is a little different from mine. Things are never going to be the same at each house, no matter how hard you try. The best you can do is pick your battles very carefully. This homework issue was one I was simply not willing to argue about. Evan got all his work done and went to bed on time. It just wasn't on the timeline I would have preferred.

These may seem like trivial situations, but they are real, likely to occur often, and can seem huge at the time. These kind of everyday issues have a great ability to drive a sharp wedge into your dual family. Don't let them! Ideally, you and your ex will be able to communicate and agree on what you want for your kids in both homes, but in reality, you know there are going to be some issues that you just won't see eye to eye on. You may never be able to adequately convey your desires for your kids to your ex, but as long as you're confident in what you're doing for your kids when they're with you, that's what counts.

There may be situations that are dangerous for your kids, so you'll need to approach these differently. Say your ex loves to ride motorcycles and doesn't make the kids wear a helmet when he takes them riding. This is obviously dangerous and can seriously harm a child if there's an accident. If you think your ex isn't making decisions in your child's best interest, then it may be time to get help from a professional.

To head off some potential problems, take a moment and think about which types of issues you and your ex are likely to butt heads on. It may help to think about which of these issues came up when you were married. Were you strict in the discipline department, but your ex was laid back? Did you require that the kids pick up their rooms and toys each night before bed but your ex didn't seem to care? Were you particular about routines and your ex was not? These are important matters to explore. Take out your journal and think about the issues you and your ex are likely to disagree about and make a list. Under each item write ways for you to deal with it. Remember, the solution may have nothing to do with your ex because you only have control over what you do. For instance, if your ex doesn't make your kids brush their teeth before they go to bed, you may be able to help the situation by teaching your kids how to brush their own teeth or by instilling in them the importance of brushing morning and night so they don't have to go through the pain of having a cavity filled later on. You might also need to take additional precautions when they are with you, like requiring extra brushing, flossing and anti-cavity rinses, and keeping less sugary items in the house. If your kids respond well to authority, having a stern talking to by the dentist may also help. That's about as much as you can do in that kind of situation, but at least now you have a few different ways to remedy the issue when your kids are with you.

Learn to look for the areas where you and your ex differ and have a hard time coming together. Keep adding to your list as time goes on, and make a list of your solutions to the problem as we did above. This will help you feel like you have a bit more control and will give you and your ex a few less issues to argue over, which is great for you, your kids, and your dual family.

Dual Family
STEPS TO SUCCESS

▸ Accept the fact that you can't control what happens when your kids are with your ex.

▸ Seek advice and help if you think your ex is putting your children in a dangerous situation that can harm them.

▸ In your journal, make a list of the kinds of issues that you and your ex are likely to differ on and write some possible solutions to each.

CHAPTER 8

SECRET #2: Let Go of Your Ego

"Big egos are big shields for lots of empty space."
—DIANA BLACK

Oh our wonderful ego! It helps us feel great about ourselves when we accomplish something wonderful, and it can easily get the better of us when we feel slighted, wronged, or taken advantage of. I've let my ego get in the way of things more than a few times. It's hard to realize it when you're in the heat of the moment, but with some time, self-awareness, and practice, you'll be able to deal with issues that arise in your dual family with a calm and level head, and leave your ego largely out of the picture.

Ego plays a role in just about every aspect of a divorce. When you go through a divorce it's easy to turn inward, just think about yourself and what you want, and let your ego take over, but that can be very dangerous not only for your dual family but for you, too. You run the risk of isolating yourself from your ex and potentially from your kids as well. No one likes to deal with an ego maniac who thinks everything is about them. An overzealous ego is a reality for everyone from time to time. Even seasoned, well-mannered dual family experts have to work to keep it under control. The key is to be aware of it and get it under control before it gets ugly.

I've mentioned numerous times that Deb, my ex-husband's wife, and I get along great. I truly like her as a person, and I greatly appreciate the way she treats my son. We've gotten along well since the day we met, and I have grown to trust and rely on her as a true partner in my dual family. So you can imagine how surprised I was recently when I had to let go of my ego and get myself under control before I made a big mistake.

Evan and his step-brother recently got braces. Grant has generally handled the dental issues for Evan, so when the time came for braces, he and Deb dealt with just about everything, from finding a doctor to scheduling appointments. So it really was no surprise that Deb was getting the appointment reminders for Evan's orthodontist appointments. I was working in my office one day when I got an email from Deb reminding me about Evan's appointment the following week. I was immediately taken aback and thought, Why is she getting reminders about my son's appointment? I'm his mother; those should be coming to me. Then it happened: My ego took over. I hit the reply button and started typing a message back to Deb asking her to have all the appointment reminders come directly to me. Maybe I was having a stressful day because this really wasn't a big deal, but I was truly miffed that she was getting these instead of me. Thank goodness a dose of reality smacked me in the head before I hit the send button. I realized I was in ego mode. I thought, Wait a minute, she's not trying to take over my duties as a mom; she's trying to help. I have one more person willing to help me; that's actually pretty great! I realized I was letting my ego take control and that it was very helpful to me to have Deb reminding me about these things. It was really quite thoughtful and kind of her to take the time to do that. Instead of writing an email back to her demanding that I get the emails from the orthodontist's office, I simply thanked her for letting me know. All was well in my happy dual family once again.

That's how easily we can lose control over such petty, silly issues. It's a little harder to gain control when the issues are bigger and cut us more deeply. Take, for instance, if your ex moves a new partner into your old house. That can hurt! It's hard enough to think of your ex with someone else but in your house, too, and with your kids, like one big, happy family. It's enough to make you want to gag and let your ego out of the bag. But before you go strutting around, making noise, and taking over the place like you still live there, ask yourself why you are feeling that way. Are you jealous of this new person? Are you still bitter that you and your ex are apart? Are you scared that your kids will like this new person better than you? That's highly unlikely, but if you're threatened by that, think about what you can do to improve your relationship with your kids instead of getting upset at this new situation. When you find your ego gets a little off track, think about the circumstances where this happens. You might need to go back and do some more work around these issues. Revisit Part 1 of the book and focus on the areas where you still have some work to do. Know that you will eventually get through this if you work at it.

It might behoove you to do some work on yourself in the broader sense too. In the course of a major life-changing event like divorce, sometimes we let our ego take control because we don't feel completely confident with who we are and what we're doing. Don't be hard on yourself if this has happened to you. With everything you have to deal with in a divorce and starting your life over again, it's expected that a few aspects of your life aren't going to be exactly what you want them to be. To change and improve these things and get you to a more confident and self-assured place, you have to deal with them head on.

Get out that journal again and ask yourself, "What am I unhappy with in my life right now, and how can I change it?" Are you unhappy with your weight? Go get some exercise, or take a walk or jog right now! I guarantee it will lift your spirits. It's even better if you can do something every day to improve your health. Are you challenged with your finances? Sit down and review your finances. Scary, I know. Create a plan to spend less and put more money in the bank. Start with something really simple like cutting out that morning cup of Starbucks and putting the $20 you would have spent there each week in the bank instead. Even something as small as that can help you feel more in control of your finances. Not happy with your job? Work on your resume, find a recruiter and network to look for a better position. Take classes at your local college if you'd like to improve your education.

Create action steps for you to move forward with some of these items. What can you do right now, tomorrow, and the rest of this week to start chipping away at this list? You can spend your whole life complaining about your circumstances and how unfair life is, but that isn't going to get you anywhere. You must take action and change things if you want improve. The best way I know to keep my ego in check is to make sure I have a full and fulfilling life because when I'm happy and confident, there isn't much other people can do that bothers me, and my ego is much more likely to stay hidden.

There are so many things you can do to make yourself feel better about yourself and your situation. When you're confident and secure in who you are and where you stand with your kids, you won't have nearly as many issues where your ego takes over, potentially wreaking havoc in your dual family.

Dual Family
STEPS TO SUCCESS

- ▸ Be aware of when your ego is getting the better of you.

- ▸ If you're taking things personally and your ego is taking over, think of why you may be feeling this way. If you still have work to do in grieving or acceptance, refer back to Part 1 and consult your vision for your happy dual family.

- ▸ List in your journal the things you can improve in your life and create an action item list to start working on them.

CHAPTER 9

SECRET #3: Stay Focused on Your Vision

"Your vision will become clear only when you look into
your heart. Who looks outside, dreams.
Who looks inside, awakens."

—CARL JUNG

Letting go of your ego will help you immensely with this secret as well. Let's go back to the reason you're here, the reason you're reading this book. Obviously you want a happier atmosphere in your divorced family, but why? Not everyone does, you know. Go back to the vision you created in Chapter 3. If you haven't quite finished it, or if you've thought of additional reasons you'd like to write down, or if you've developed your thoughts more completely, finish writing them now. Moving forward you'll want the most complete version of why you're doing all this work. I suggest you keep a written copy of your vision for your dual family in a place where you can refer to it regularly, at least in the beginning, like maybe a bed stand where you can read it before you go to bed at night. You may also want to keep a copy in your car or your desk at work, or anywhere you can easily access it when you need to. It takes a while to get really good at dealing with the ups and downs of your dual family without having to refer to your vision for direction. With enough focus and practice though, it becomes second nature, and you'll carry your vision in your heart and in your head instead of in your pocket.

Referring to your vision will help keep your ego in check, too. When it starts to run amuck, and it will from time to time, reflecting on *why* you want to be in a happy and cooperative dual family will help you take the appropriate actions to ensure you walk a steady path to your goal and keep your ego in line.

My ego ran amuck a few years ago, and my vision was immensely helpful to keep my actions in line with my goals. When the stock market crashed in 2008, so did my income, as was the case with so many people. I had lost money in my investment accounts, but more important, my day-to-day income was affected dramatically. I had to drastically change the way we lived. No more house cleaner, eating out, or new clothes—you get the point. Evan was a trooper. He didn't mind that we had to cut back. We had fun at home instead of going on vacation, and trips to the library replaced expensive trips to the bookstore.

I happened to be watching a financial report on CNBC one morning. Not a great way to start your morning when the markets are collapsing. The outlook for the economy and my industry was looking worse by the hour. The total collapse of our economy didn't seem far off. I started to get very nervous, and I remembered the one thing I had agreed to in our divorce settlement that I wished I hadn't. Reluctantly, I agreed to trade off having Evan as a tax deduction every other year. Tax season was around the corner, and as I became more concerned about the state of the U.S. economy and mine, I thought about how helpful that extra money would be. This was not my year to have him as a deduction, but I thought if I explained the situation to Grant, surely he would have some sympathy and allow me to take the deduction this year, too. He and his wife both had good salaries and they had her boys as deductions so it couldn't hurt too much, right? The more I thought about it, the more relief it brought me. Hopeful and a little more encouraged, I called Grant to discuss this with him, fully expecting him to oblige and say yes. What I got was a flat out no! He said they had been affected as well and just couldn't swing it. He proceeded to run me through all the reasons they couldn't give up the deduction this year. I was floored. That wasn't the answer I had expected. I had lost a huge percentage of my income in just one year and now my hope of keeping just a tiny bit more of it had been trashed.

I turned back to the CNBC program and became more and more fearful with the dire news. I allowed my fear to turn to anger against Grant. I started to get mad. I could feel my blood pressure rising by the minute as I thought about all the things I gave up in our divorce to keep our family happy. I didn't ask for child support or alimony. I gave up my house and most of the things in it. I didn't go after his pension. Now, the one time I actually ask for something, he has the nerve to deny me! I didn't even want to agree to trade off the tax deduction in the first place, but I felt pressured by him to do it. By the time I was done remembering all the things I gave up, I was furious. I even thought about hiring an attorney. I'll show you, I thought. I'll hire an attorney and get more than that damn tax deduction. He'll be sorry he ever said no to me!

Then it hit me. I realized what I was doing. It was like a switch flipped, the light turned on, and it lit a bright light squarely on my vision. I took a deep breath and was horrified at what I had been thinking and at how angry I was. I quickly turned off the TV and sat down. I rationalized the situation and referred back to my vision for my family.

I knew I couldn't get an attorney to fight Grant about this. First, I did agree, however reluctantly, to trade off the deduction with Grant and going to court now likely wouldn't change a darn thing. It would be an expensive, emotionally draining, and negative experience, and would likely cause a huge rift in the happy dual family I had worked so hard for years to create. I knew I was temporarily giving into my fears and what I needed to do was to stop, think, and focus on my vision. I knew if I did anything irrational like try to fight in court about this, my happy dual family would be over as would my great relationship with Deb, and Evan would be severely affected as well, living between two quarreling families. That wasn't what I wanted at all. This happened about eight years after Grant and I had separated. It just goes to show that even a seasoned dual family can have challenges that will threaten the fabric of the family unit.

Looking back, it was a good lesson for me. I was reminded to not give in to my fears. I needed to look at each situation logically and rationally with the all the facts laid out and my ego and emotions put aside. When you've learned to do this easily and consistently, you'll pretty much have mastered the use of your vision. You'll have laser focus on your vision. It will guide you to making the right decisions without you even thinking much about it, and it will carry you through the scrutiny that others might place on you because of the decisions you make. You'll be confident and content knowing that the decisions you make are for the benefit of your children, your family, and you. Your vision will be strong, and you will be, too. You, your children, and your dual family will benefit immensely from this. The more you work on it and the more focused you are, the easier and more natural it becomes. Hang in there during the tough times. With your vision as your guide, you'll learn to pull yourself through them, and you'll be living a much happier life.

When you come across a difficult situation with your ex, just ask yourself these questions: How will my decision affect my relationship with my ex now and in the long run? If I choose to handle the situation this way, will my dual family be better or worse off tomorrow? Is this course of action in line with my vision for my happy dual family? What actions can I take to handle the situation that will help my dual family and will be in line with my vision? Answering these questions honestly will help you make the right decisions. When you stick to your vision, swallow your pride when needed, let go of your ego, and focus on your family, you just can't go wrong.

Dual Family
STEPS TO SUCCESS

▸ If you haven't completed your vision for your happy dual family or you want to add to it, do so now.

▸ Keep a printed copy of your vision anywhere you might need to access it.

▸ Read your vision every day until it becomes second nature to you.

▸ In difficult situations, ask yourself if the way you are dealing with them is helping or hurting your dual family and find positive ways to best deal with the issues that are in line with your vision.

CHAPTER 10

SECRET #4: Don't Keep Score

"Keeping score of old scores and scars, getting even and one-upping always make you less than you are."
—MALCOLM FORBES

This can be so incredibly hard to do. You're already mad at your ex for at least a dozen reasons, and now he keeps making the same dumb mistakes, and you're not supposed to notice? What's up with that? How is *that* fair? Well, it's fair when you realize just how much it can hurt you, your kids, and your dual family.

I have a friend Jeremy who's going through a divorce. He and his soon-to-be ex-wife don't have kids, but they have two dogs he brought into the relationship. They both love and adore the pups, and each of them wants to have the dogs full time. Sound familiar? So they agreed each of them would have a couple of days with the pups, just like many people do with their kids.

Don't think for a second that all the challenges in a dual family revolve around the kids. The tribulations and trials of divorce know no boundaries whether human, canine, feline or other. He was lamenting to me the other night about how his ex was getting mad at him for picking the dogs up late (like they even know or care, right?). He's a real estate broker, and his schedule changes daily. He certainly tries to be on time, but if an appointment runs long or a great opportunity drops in his lap, he needs to take advantage of it, and that can cause him to be late in picking up the pups.

Jeremy's ex makes a point of keeping score and noting every time he's late picking up the dogs. She thinks he should try harder to be there at the prearranged time. As he's telling me this, I'm thinking, They're dogs! If she has to leave, they can stay in the yard or the garage until he gets to the house to pick them up. It certainly doesn't need to inconvenience her and her schedule. It's not as if they need a babysitter like children do, so what the heck is she complaining about? But see, this is what we do, even with pets. Even when the issue involves an animal that can't possibly be aware that there even is an issue, we can create one—just for fun. We gripe, complain, and nitpick until we feel we've made our point, and even sometimes after that. Maybe it's for a sense of control or maybe your ex just wants to make you mad for some reason. For some people, negative communication is better than no communication at all.

You see, though, this type of power playing and jockeying for control doesn't do you any good. Sure, it might feel good in the moment. You may feel you've made your point or that you've stuck it to your ex one more time, but that breeds something very dangerous that can't easily be undone: resentment. It's hard to be friendly and cooperative for the benefit of your dual family when you're keeping score at the same time. Keep up that kind of behavior, and in no time at all, your ex won't want to cooperate with you in any way, shape, or form. Soon, you'll get angry that your ex isn't quite as easy to deal with as she used to be, and it can snowball downhill from there.

This not only affects you but your kids as well. They can sense when there's tension in the family. This is stressful for children. They might not know what's going on, but they'll know it doesn't feel good. Not to mention the fact that when you're score-keeping, you're obviously bothered and upset, and you're much more likely to blurt out something negative and terribly inappropriate to your kids.

Try to avoid keeping score at all costs. No one is perfect. We all make mistakes, including you. Yes, my dear, your time will come when you need some understanding and support from your ex, and you certainly aren't going to want your constant criticism and griping thrown back at you. To not receive it, the best thing you can do is not dish it out in the first place. Make sense? The next time you want to keep score about something and complain to your ex about it, bite your tongue instead. If you need to talk about it with someone, do not turn to your kids; go to a positive friend who can help you put the right spin on things and get you back into dual family focus. If your issue involves pets, though, and you want to gripe to them about it, let it rip. I don't think they'll know the difference.

Let's look at another example. What if your ex works odd hours and can't regularly take the kids to their sporting events on time, so you frequently have to jump in at the last minute? What you don't want to do in this situation is throw it back at your ex, and say something like "Why can't you take the kids to football practice on time? You've been late three times in a row, and I've had to do it at the last minute. Can't you be on time?" Let's be realistic about this. That kind of attitude isn't going to make your ex want to snap to it and be on time from now on, is it? Of course not. Instead, approach the situation with a spirit of cooperation and say something more cooperative and helpful like "I know it's hard for you to pick up the kids and take them to practice, so how about I take them to practice and you pick them up? That way, the kids are on time, you still get to spend some time with them a little later in the day, and I don't have to change my schedule at the last minute if something comes up for you. Would that work better with your schedule?" Wow! After he picks his jaw up off the floor, how is your ex going to feel about partnering with you in a dual family? Probably pretty darn good, right? With this approach, it's much more likely your ex will put forth some extra effort to make the new arrangements work well.

This is how a happy dual family acts. It's cooperative, generous, and giving whenever possible. When you need some help, your ex is much more likely to extend to you the same kindness in return. You might think that giving so generously to your ex is going to be really hard, and it might be the first few times. If your ex has hurt you deeply, it isn't easy to be kind and generous. But with some time and a little bit of giving, it gets easier, and you'll feel better about it. In fact, once you've had enough practice, you're likely to do it almost without even realizing it.

Remember, you aren't really doing this just to be nice; it's actually a little bit selfish. You're doing this for you so you don't have to live in a world of negativity and stress with your ex. Of course, you're also doing this for your kids. How happy are your kids going to be without the negativity and complaining associated with criticizing your ex constantly? It never makes the kids feel good, happy, or safe to know that mom and dad are fighting, whether you live under one roof or two. They're going to be much happier, more secure, be more open to you as a parent, and they're likely to perform better at sports and in school. Your life will absolutely improve the more you get along with your ex. I'd be willing to swallow a little pride and reach out a helping hand to my ex any day to get those kinds of results, wouldn't you?

Dual Family
STEPS TO SUCCESS

- ▸ Don't keep score when your ex does something wrong.

- ▸ To release your frustrations, instead of keeping score, talk with a positive friend about it, but avoid discussing it with your kids.

- ▸ If you're having a persistent issue with your ex, like being consistently late to pick up the kids, look for positive solutions you can offer to your ex.

CHAPTER 11

SECRET #5: Manipulation Is
Never Allowed

*"Love comes when manipulation stops, when you think
more about the other person than about his or her
reactions to you. When you dare to reveal yourself fully.
When you dare to be vulnerable."*
—DR. JOYCE BROTHERS

Miriam Webster's Dictionary defines manipulation as "to influence, especially with intent to deceive." Let's look at some other words associated with deception and manipulation. How about misleading, false, shady, devious, shifty, sneaky, and underhanded? Now, I have to ask you, do you truly want your behavior to be associated with any of these words or for your children to be exposed to that type of behavior? I'm fairly certain you don't.

Manipulation can happen so easily and quickly, we don't even completely realize we're doing it, and we don't always know the impact it will have on us or our kids. Unfortunately in our society, manipulation is terribly common. Where is the truth and reality if you're trying to make things happen a certain way or trying to get someone wrapped around your finger just so you can get them to do what you want, whether they want to do it or not?

For the one being deceived, it can be easy to fall victim to someone who's so crafty. This rarely turns out well though, for either party. The manipulator continues to live a life of deception without a firm connection to reality, and the person being manipulated usually gets shafted and hurt. None of this is model behavior for your kids, and it certainly doesn't belong in the lives of your children. Kids learn by example. If you're exemplifying manipulation, you better watch out! Kids are fast studies and are likely to be even better at it than you. That's a scary thought!

Sheila has to deal with a controlling and manipulative ex on a regular basis. She told me about a particular issue where her daughter was put right in the middle of her and her ex, and it caused her quite a bit of stress. Belinda, her daughter, loved to skateboard every day. It was her favorite sport and latest passion. She spent hours riding up and down the street, jumping off curbs, and testing her skills at the skate park. In fact, she used the skateboard so much that it broke. Sheila wasn't quite sure how Belinda would like skateboarding when she bought her a board to try out, so she didn't buy the highest-quality board and felt terrible when it broke after only a few months of use. So they went to the local skateboard shop and bought a great board that Belinda loved. Belinda was beaming with excitement as they brought the new board home and she took it out for its maiden run. It was perfect, and she couldn't have been happier. That didn't last long, though. As soon as Sheila's ex found out about the new skateboard, he flipped. You would think that getting something that made their child happy and fueled her passion for sports and exercise would have been a good thing for everyone. But it wasn't.

Her ex wasn't at all happy with the new skateboard. He's very frugal and likes to teach that same trait to his daughter. He would have preferred for the skateboard to have been bought on Craigslist or for her to get a used one instead of an expensive new one. He may have even been a little miffed because he wanted to be the parent who bought the skateboard. Whatever the reason, he wasn't happy and he called Shelia several times to ask her to take the board back. Of course, Sheila refused. Calling her to tell her to take the board back was a little over the line, but he crossed into the manipulation zone when he brought their daughter into the mix.

This happens all the time and it's easy to do, so remember this example and try to see this in your own situations. He wasn't getting the results he wanted from Sheila, so he turned to his child to deal with the issue. He told Belinda that she had to take the skateboard back or he would take it back the next time he saw it. He was using his child to get the result he wanted from Sheila. Just imagine what was going through that child's mind. Imagine the stress she must have felt being put in the middle of two parents she loves very much and wants to please but are both telling her different things. That's a lot of unnecessary pressure to put on a child. Kids want to please both parents, and you put them in a very difficult place when you try and get them to deal with an issue they clearly shouldn't be involved with. This was a situation for Sheila and her ex to handle, not their daughter. Manipulating your kids and putting them in the middle of yourself and your ex is wrong. Be an adult and talk with your ex yourself.

Unfortunately, the difficulties with the skateboard lasted for weeks. Belinda was so distraught and stressed by the whole thing, she gave up her new sport all together. The thing she loved most quickly became something she couldn't stand to deal with anymore. It didn't have to be that way, though. Had Sheila's ex simply resigned himself to the fact that Belinda got a new skateboard and didn't make a fuss over it, she would still happily be skateboarding and having fun, just as she should be.

It's not only the kids who can be manipulated. Adults can be easily manipulated as well. Avoid trying to control or influence your ex. Getting what you want by manipulating others isn't going to help you or your family in the long run. Face situations with composure, maturity, and fairness. I know it isn't always easy to do, but it's the right thing to do. It's the same for friends and family members. It just can't be tolerated. Be truthful and fair instead of trying to get your way or what you want. Being honest with yourself and others goes a long way toward creating a happy dual family. Look for instances where you might try to find a way to get what you want, especially when it involves getting other people to do something to further your goal. We don't always see it in ourselves when we manipulate, so you have to look for it. With some practice, you may be able to see it more clearly. It's the same with other people in your life. If you have a family member who tries to manipulate you, your ex, or your kids for whatever reason, recognize it and put a stop to it. Just come right out and say or ask for what you want or need. This is a far simpler and less dramatic way of dealing with a situation and much more healthy for everyone involved.

To assist you in dealing with issues like the one above, I'm going to point you back to your vision. Ask yourself, Is putting your child in the middle of you and your ex really what you want for your kids? We don't always get what we want, especially when it comes to our ex. You're going to lose some battles, maybe a lot of them, but that's fine. You don't truly lose the battle if your kids are happy and left alone to be kids. We always win when we do right by our children and do what's necessary to keep them happy, safe, and emotionally secure. You just have to look at "winning" an issue a little differently.

Dual Family
STEPS TO SUCCESS

- ▸ Don't manipulate your kids or your ex to get what you want.

- ▸ Don't put your kids in between you and your ex or get them to fight your battles for you.

- ▸ Look for areas and issues where you may try to manipulate your ex or children, and think of healthier ways to reach your desired outcome.

- ▸ Refer back to your vision to ensure you're handling issues according to your values and vision for your dual family.

CHAPTER 12

SECRET #6: Don't Play the Victim
or Talk Badly About Your Ex

*"It's all right to sit on your pity pot every now and again.
Just be sure to flush when you're finished."*
—DEBBIE MACOMBER

Playing the victim is just as dangerous as being manipulated or being manipulative, and is a form of manipulation itself. It can manifest in many ways, but it ultimately comes down to the way you think about a situation and how you see yourself in it. In a healthy point of view, you are part of your circumstances; when you play the victim, you feel as though things happen to you.

Perhaps a parent thinks he's the victim in his divorce because his wife and kids moved out of the house and to another city, leaving him alone. He feels betrayed, lonely, sad, and abandoned. He doesn't take into account the fact that his wife left with the kids because he was abusive to her and undermined their marriage. He may go around telling people and truly believing himself that all he did was love her deeply. He can't understand why she left and why they can't be a family. This self-produced victim image is not only damaging for him because he won't be able to change his behavior to a more healthy form unless he can clearly see his negative actions, but it can hurt his children, too.

The image he portrays to his kids by being needy and having a poor-me attitude will not help them. If you play the victim, it allows your children to feel as if they need to take care of you, instead of you taking care of them. In effect, the child becomes the parent. As a parent, you should always be the bigger, stronger person.

Have you ever noticed that people who play the victim can't stop talking about every little thing that's wrong in their lives? They can't wait to tell everyone about it! It feels great to let everyone know what a terrible state they're in so we all can feel badly for them. They'll even tell their kids. Let's say a mom complains she's in such hard times that her electricity got cut off because she hasn't paid her bill. With a victim mentality she tells everyone how terrible it was to have no power to cook the kids dinner, how cold they were until she got the power turned back on, and that she can't believe anyone would turn off the power to a house with children in it. How could this have happened to her? She makes no mention, however, that she wasn't able to pay her bill because she bought a very expensive pair of shoes and she didn't really think they would turn off the power. From her twisted point of view, which may be very real and true in her mind, this problem happened to her. In reality, though, she took part in her own circumstances, and that's that way it is quite often in divorce and in life. Sure, sometimes things do happen to us, but quite often, we're a part of it in some way or another.

Ask yourself, do you ever play the victim? Do you feel that you're wronged through no fault of your own? Be honest with yourself; no one is perfect. The objective is to recognize and understand our mistakes so we can work to improve them. These kinds of things can be hard to see in ourselves, so it may help to get out your journal and write down the things that you feel you've been victimized and wronged by. Then think about and write down what you could have done differently to avoid or change the outcome.

Take this example. Your ex is supposed to pay you child support every month but often doesn't; in fact, he has a track record of not paying more times than he's paid it. The victim will blame her ex for everything she doesn't have and can't afford without looking at what part she may have played in her financial situation. While she has every right to be upset about him not making his promised monthly payments, she doesn't consider the fact that when she received her divorce settlement, she bought a rather pricey sports car with a monthly payment of $650 a month. He may not be paying her, but she has a role to play in her financial situation as well. Look on your list to see where you can take control to improve less-than-perfect areas in your life. I know it isn't fun to look at these things; it's much easier to blame others and feel victimized, but that won't change your circumstances and improve your life. If you want a better life, you have to stop playing the victim and take control.

In the case of divorce, often we communicate to our children that we've been victimized by talking badly about our ex in front of them. Now to be fair, your ex may be a real jerk. She may be manipulative and controlling and drive you absolutely to the edge of the earth, but that doesn't mean you get to talk badly about her in front of your kids. No matter how much you'd like to scream from the rooftop that your ex is a no-good, low-life, cheating, lying piece of crap, don't do it around your kids. Kids love both their parents, and they don't want to hear the parent they love being talked about so poorly. It hurts them. You may be trying to hurt your ex by disparaging them, but when you do it in front of your kids, it just harms them, and it doesn't make you look all that great, either.

Instead of talking badly to others about your ex, write how you feel in your journal. Be as nasty as you like and get it all out. Remember those positivity partners I mentioned before? It's always good to rely on a friend who you can speak openly and honestly with, and because they're your positivity partner and know what you're trying to accomplish with your dual family, they'll more than likely help you put a positive spin on things.

Putting that positive spin on things is very important. We create our own reality by our thoughts, and when we speak our thoughts and act on our them, they become even more real. The more you think about your ex and what a miserable mess she is, the more you reinforce those thoughts. Work with your positive friends and family to help you shift your thoughts. I'm not saying you need to start thinking she's wonderful, but at some point you loved that person enough to marry them. Try to look for the positives and not focus on the negatives. This will help you not feel like a victim and feel better about your ex so you aren't as likely to talk badly about them.

Remember, playing the victim and talking badly about your ex doesn't hurt them; it hurts you and your kids. Initially, the kids may buy into the victim role and feel sorry for the victimized parent and give them more attention or want to help them, but kids are smart and will figure it out. Once they realize you've played that card, playing the victim will eventually hurt your relationship with your kids. They lose respect for you. Be strong, be honest with your kids, and you'll all be much happier for it.

Dual Family
STEPS TO SUCCESS

▸ Don't play the victim.

▸ Write in your journal about areas of your life where you feel victimized, then think of ways you can change the situation.

▸ Don't talk badly about your ex.

▸ Rely on your positivity partners to help you shift your negative thoughts about your ex to more positive ones.

CHAPTER 13

SECRET #7: Bond With Your Kids

"Romance fails us and so do friendships, but the relationship of parent and child, less noisy than all the others, remains indelible and indestructible, the strongest relationship on earth."
—THEODORE REIK

This is my favorite secret by far! It's easy to let the experience of divorce shake your self-assuredness. When you divorce, your world can change dramatically and you realize the happy path you were walking with your partner has come to an abrupt end. It can shake the confidence of even the most assured among us. My confidence has been shaken many times. It feels terrible, and unless you have a method to come out of it, it can begin to leak into various aspects of your life. The way I generally handle this issue as well as others that tend to make me feel bad or unhappy is to deepen and grow my relationship with my son. It is what grounds me, makes me happier than anything else I can experience, and it never fails to pull me out of any funk I might be in. Take every advantage to bond with your kids as often as you can. There are probably dozens of opportunities to bond with your kids every day, but too often we're so busy and preoccupied, we miss many of them.

I remember one time Evan came upstairs to my office while I was busy working and asked me to come downstairs to be with him for a while. I was too focused on work and told him that I just couldn't right now because I had too much to do. He walked away with his head down and his shoulders slumped over in disappointment. I felt terrible as I watched him walk away. He was reaching out to me for love and attention, and I had totally blown him off. I took a deep breath, pushed myself away from my desk and told him I would stop working for a few minutes to just be with him. He beamed with delight!

That was a bonding moment. They're critical in keeping our relationship strong, open, and delightfully happy. Most parents don't describe their relationship with their kids as delightfully happy, but mine truly is. I attribute Evan's good behavior and our strong relationship to the many opportunities we've had to bond with each other over the years. I believe every parent and child have the ability to create this special relationship with each other. It just takes some effort.

I asked some friends who I consider great parents and have respectful and loving relationships with their kids what they do to bond with their children. Here's a sampling. You can try any of these. They aren't expensive or hard. You just have to create the opportunity, and do it.

- Eat dinner together every night without the TV on. Talk and connect with each other.
- Take a walk after dinner with no electronic devices. Just talk.

- Make a special breakfast on the weekend so your kids always look forward to it, and make sure to eat together. We make breakfast for dinner once a week. It's a fun treat and easy after a busy workday.
- Take a day hike or bike ride on the weekends. Make it something you can regularly look forward to.
- Treat your children as equals. Don't talk down to them. Respect their opinions, wants, and needs.
- Take some time at night to talk and recap the day and just cuddle. It will send both of you off to sleep feeling happy and content. Do something sweet like rub your child's back and tell them you love them more than anything.
- Spend some time in the morning waking your kids up with kisses, a smile, and hugs, instead of an alarm clock.
- Allow your kids to speak freely without fear of being judged. Make sure they know they can come to you for anything without being afraid of what you'll say or do.
- Find some special things that you and your kids like to do together, whether it's building something, reading, playing a game, swimming, or biking together.
- When your kids are having problems, instead of telling them what to do, tell them how you dealt with a similar situation at their age.
- Have a family day every week to do something special together. If you can't do a whole day, do an evening or a few hours.
- Take time to truly stop and listen to your kids and give them what they need.
- Be affectionate with your kids. Lots of hugs and kisses and I love yous.

- Create nicknames for each other that you don't use for anyone else.
- Take an interest in what they like even if you don't. You child might love bugs. Get them a bug kit or watch a movie on bugs together. Help your kids explore their passions.

You might be divorced, but you and your kids are still a family, and you have a great opportunity to build some fun family memories and very strong bonds. For Evan and me, it's all about respect for each other, open communication that's not judgmental, trust, and oodles of love. We are 12 years into our bond now, and I can honestly say it's grown stronger every year.

On my absolute worst days, all I have to do is get a warm hug and kiss from Evan, and my world is right. When you're arguing with your ex and not feeling so great about your dual family, your bond with your kids will help pull you through.

Take a moment to make a list in your journal of some ways you can bond more closely with your kids on a regular basis, and be sure to ask them what they think you can do to be closer as a family, too. Commit to doing at least one new thing each day you are with them, and incorporate things like eating dinner together each night or reading together at bedtime into your regular routine. Before long you will be doing many things that will bond you more closely to your kids every day.

Dual Family
S TEPS TO S UCCESS

▸ Every day look for ways you can bond more closely with your kids.

▸ Make a list in your journal of things you can do regularly to bond more closely with your kids.

▸ Commit to doing one new thing each day to bond with your kids.

▸ Incorporate certain things like a weekly movie night or eating dinner together into your regular routine.

CHAPTER 14

SECRET #8: Find a Positive Accountability Partner

"If you hang out with chickens, you're going to cluck, and if you hang out with eagles, you're going to fly."
—STEVE MARABOLI

It's so critical to have at least one person you can trust to be in your corner and be able to keep you on track with your happy dual family. There will be times you're going to be incredibly angry with your ex, the family isn't moving in the right direction, and your vision will seemingly be destroyed right in front of you. It's enough to make you want to give up on the idea of a happy dual family, get angry, and fight it out with your ex. There will also be times when you're going to feel very lonely, downtrodden and depressed, and question everything you're doing and why. It's during these times that you need someone to remind you exactly why you're doing what you're doing. Why you're going through all this heartache, why you've given up so much, and what's waiting for you on the other side.

I had three friends who helped me through my most troubled times after my divorce. All of them offered a shoulder to cry on and an ear to bend. I remember sitting on my couch in my tiny studio apartment when Evan was with his dad one night. I missed him so much. I felt terribly alone and was questioning everything. I was in tears when I called one of my trusted friends and she encouraged me and helped me regain focus on my plan. She reassured me I was a fantastic mom, that I would get through my struggles with Grant, and that Evan was happy. Her calming voice, love, and commitment to my success was exactly what I needed to see me through the tough times.

Unfortunately, many people are negative, so what will often happen is that family, friends, and co-workers will try to show their support for you by bad-mouthing your ex or telling you to fight it out in court and get what you deserve, as well as myriad other things that may be in direct conflict with your vision for your happy dual family. Right now, you don't need someone telling you what a witch your ex is, how irresponsible he is, or that you should be getting more money from alimony or child support. All those things may very well be true, but they don't need to be reiterated to you. When you start hearing the negative things, it's natural that your mind will start focusing in that direction, and once you start down that negative path, it's hard to stop. Hearing lots of negative things from those around you will only reinforce and escalate the negative banter in your head. Get rid of that negative mindset about your ex and replace it with one of acceptance, tolerance, patience, and cooperation. There are people who can help you build on those positive feelings toward your ex; you just need to find them and ask for their help.

Just like in marriage, we don't always do a great job of communicating with our family and friends. There are lots of different reasons for this; we may assume the other person already understands what we want, or perhaps we think they'll figure it out. Maybe we just don't quite know how to put our thoughts or feelings into words. We might be a little nervous to ask for specific help or of what the other person might think or say about what we want. All of this can lead to misunderstanding. This is a fragile time, though, and the last thing you need is more misunderstanding in your life. There's probably plenty of that already. Be open, honest, and direct about your needs and desires. Sure, you might not get what you want every time, but at least you've asked for it, and that's more than most people would do, so you're already ahead of the curve.

If a family member doesn't want to be supportive about your desire to not bad-mouth your ex, that's OK, just steer clear of them as much as possible until you're in a solid place with your ex and you're firmly on the path to your happy dual family. If a particular friend isn't interested in being a positivity partner, find another person to rely on. You're in a period of growth here, and you need to openly and clearly ask for what you want from those around you, in addition to their help and support to achieve it.

Take a minute and think about what you'd like in a positivity partner. Would you like someone to simply tell you you're doing a great job all the time who will reiterate that your ex has good intentions and remind you to be understanding? Someone you can just vent to when you get really miffed at your ex? What is it that would help you stay on your path to getting along better with your ex?

Grab your journal again and write these things down. Include how often you'd like to request help from or speak with your positivity partner. Would you prefer to speak as needed, when a problem arises, or would it be more helpful to have consistent, positive reinforcement? Everyone is different, so think about what would be most helpful to you, and write it down as completely as you can so you'll be able to ask for it and have a high likelihood of getting it.

Once you've thought about what you want, think about who the ideal people are to give it to you. List a few of your family members and friends whom you trust and speak with often. Choose two or three people from each list you think will be great positive people, who'll support and encourage you as you develop your happy dual family. With anyone you see or speak with regularly, not just those you are seeking as positivity partners, you want to make sure you communicate your desire for getting along with your ex and ask for their cooperation and support. This will make it just that much easier for you and grow your positivity bubble just a little bigger.

When you approach a potential positivity partner and ask for their assistance, take some time to explain why you're speaking with them about this and why you think they'll be a great person to help keep you on task with your new family dynamic. More than likely that person will be flattered that you thought so highly of them and will be happy to help. Be sure to clearly define what you're looking for from them, and ask them if that will work for them. It doesn't need to be a formal or heavy conversation, but you do need to ask for what you want. It may go something like this:

"Jake, you know I've been working hard on getting along with Isabel so we can still have a happy family after the divorce, but it isn't always easy. You're one of my most positive friends, and I was hoping you could help me from time to time."

"Of course! Anything you need. How can I help?"

"Well, when Isabel does something to make me mad, and it makes me want to fight with her, I'd like to be able to call you and have you help pull me back in a more positive direction, to remind me why I'm working so hard to get along with her and about all the good things she's done so I'm in a better place."

"Oh, sure, no problem. I can absolutely do that for you. You know, she really does have a good heart."

"Thanks! I knew I could count on you. It'll be a lot easier for me to get along with her if I have your help."

"I'm here whenever you need me. Don't hesitate to call. And you know, you're doing a great job with the kids, too."

The conversation can be as simple as that. Now you have a partner to help you stay focused in a positive direction, they know what you need, and you know how to get it. The more of these people you have, the better. This won't last forever. You may only need a positivity partner until you're strong and successful enough to focus on your goals and vision on your own. With practice and consistent awareness on your vision, it will become second nature to make the right decisions. Until then, these positivity partners will be invaluable in helping you achieve your goals and will make the inevitable difficult times you'll face much easier to deal with.

Dual Family
STEPS TO SUCCESS

▸ Look for the most positive people in your life, and try to step away from the negative ones.

▸ Write in your journal about what kind of support you'd like from a positivity partner, the kinds of reinforcement you want from them, and how often you'd like to speak to them.

▸ Create a list of potential partners, and recruit them to help you.

CHAPTER 15

SECRET #9: Write a Contract

"It's learning how to negotiate to keep both sides happy,
whether it's for a multimillion-dollar contract or just
which show to watch on TV, that determines
the quality and enjoyment of our lives."
—LEIGH STEINBERG

I mentioned the contract earlier in the book. You may or may not be at the point with your ex where you can sit down and discuss the details of what you'd like your new dual family situation to look and feel like. If you are at that point, bravo! You now have a fantastic opportunity for you and your ex to formally agree on how you want to deal with certain issues within your dual family. If you're not at that point, don't despair. You can still write a contract for how you'd ideally like your dual family to be. You'll just be doing it for yourself. Your ex may or may not even know that you've done this, but it doesn't really matter. When you do it, even just for you, you'll firmly know the direction you'll want your family to go, and you'll be more likely to make that happen because you've created a contract stating it. You've heard the saying that those who write down their goals are more likely to achieve them? Writing a contract for how you want the ins and outs of your dual family to function is along those same lines.

What exactly do you put in your contract? What's the purpose of it? This is a contract between you and your ex detailing how you want to deal with certain issues with your kids and each other, and it will also incorporate a bit of your vision as well. For instance, if your vision includes spending your children's birthdays together as a family, your contract will outline how that will happen. If having open and free communication with your kids while they're with your ex is part of your vision, your contract with your ex might state that you both can call the children each day between 8 am and 8 pm to chat.

You want to tackle the most common, everyday issues as well as the ones that are most venomous and likely to disturb the fabric of your dual family. It's a list of statements you both agree to abide by. Since every family's issues are different, you'll need to make a list of what's most important to you and your family. These are generally day-to-day issues that may not be covered in your divorce agreement. Here are some examples:

- Will the schedule for the kids going back and forth to each parent be fluid or consistent?
- When is the right time to introduce the kids to a new partner?
- Will the bedtime/homework/chore routines be the same at each house or different?
- How are birthdays and holidays going to be handled?
- Who's going to pay for things like new school clothes, shoes, haircuts, etc.?
- Will you still get together as a family, and how often will that be?

- Can you agree on the number and type of after-school activities for each child? Who's responsible for deciding on that and paying for them?
- Will both parents commit to living locally and taking an active role in the family?
- Can you agree to only date people who are emotionally healthy and good role models for the kids?
- If one of you disapproves of or is upset about how something is being handled in the family, how will you deal with that?
- Can you both commit to giving each other your best and creating a cohesive dual family?
- Can you agree to put the happiness of your family first?

There are dozens of different issues you can put into the contract. Try to focus on the larger issues and not nitpick too much. Think about what the deal breakers are for you in your family and what you'd truly like to accomplish. You can certainly add to the contract as time goes on, too. The point is to be able to reference it in tough times and remind your ex what you're working toward and what's really important. When times get really tough, this can be a lifesaver.

You can also add items that might just pertain to you and your new household and have nothing to do with your ex. You're starting a new chapter in your life, so if you hated that your ex paid your kids an allowance but never had them do chores for it, now's your time to change that. Do you want to keep yourself on track for certain things with your kids like no television or technology during dinner or making sure you schedule one charity event that you and your kids participate in together every year? Write it all down in your contract. It's your cheat sheet for your new life.

I don't know about you but I love lists! I love making a list, reviewing it days later, and knowing with satisfaction that I made some real accomplishments. It's a great feeling! This is a list you can refer to regularly. Keep it on your refrigerator, your bathroom mirror, or your bedside table where you can refer to it every day to ensure you're working in the right direction. For more ideas on writing a contract and a sample contract you can download, go to the Resources page on www.DualFamily.com/book-resources.

Dual Family
STEPS TO SUCCESS

▸ Think of the most critical issues for your family and some of the most common issues you think you'll be dealing with.

▸ Incorporate the goals from your vision where needed.

▸ Write a contract that outlines how you and your ex will handle each of these issues.

▸ If you're on good enough terms with your ex, discuss the contract with him or her and get their buy-in.

▸ If you aren't on good terms with your ex yet, you can write a contract for your own household and for yourself to keep you on track and to ensure your family is moving in the right direction.

▸ Keep the contract somewhere where you can refer to it regularly and read it often to remind yourself of your goals.

PART 4

It Really *Is* All About You!

"You cannot afford to live in potential for the rest of your life; at some point, you have to unleash the potential and make your move."

—ERIC THOMAS

I've mentioned a few times that this process is all about you. It's not about getting your ex to do what you want them to, making your kids want to be with you more than your ex, or outdoing your ex—it's about you. It's a process to help you discover more about who you are and who you want to become. When you have the opportunity divorce brings you to start over, what will you do with it? Do you want to go back, as much as possible, to the life you had before your divorce, or reinvent your life and make it into something bolder and more beautiful? Do you want to be the same person you were in your relationship, or grow, change, and develop? Whichever direction you choose to take is completely up to you, not your ex. This is *your* life now, and that's what this part of the book is about: *you*!

I realize you may be reading this and thinking all this happy dual family stuff is a little pie-in-the-sky, and it may work just fine for some people but not for you and your ex, and you're right. This won't work for every divorced couple. Not every person is big enough and strong enough to put their ego aside and put their family first. If this is your situation, then you must take charge and move forward to a happy family your way. Just because your ex can't or doesn't want to be part of a happy dual family doesn't mean you can't work toward the wonderful, happy family goals on your own. You may need to do this if your ex is just too difficult to get along with, and let's face it, we know that type is out there, or if your ex simply doesn't want to have anything to do with you or your children anymore. If you're facing either of these scenarios, you can work to overcome them, and I'll show you how.

Once you've gone through all the hard work and your family is settled and happy, you're comfortable in your new single life, and your children are content, what are you going to do? What are you going to change in your life for *you*? We're not talking about the kids and the family anymore; this is where I want you to be just a little selfish and think of all the amazing possibilities that are in front of you. I want you to get out of living day by day and start living your dreams and designing your best life! The world will open up for you if you ask it to, but it's not going to knock on your door and wait for you to open it. You have to take the lead here, and I promise you, once you do, your life will never be the same.

This is the most exciting part of the book for me, and I hope for you, too. You've already laid the groundwork for developing a great family after your divorce; now it's time to lay the groundwork for your life, to create a plan and start making it happen. Whether you want to learn to fly an airplane, start your own company, or sing and dance on stage, you can make that happen—and it starts here.

CHAPTER 16

When It's Not So Easy

"When we long for life without difficulties, remind us
that oaks grow strong in contrary winds and
diamonds are made under pressure."
—PETER MARSHALL

I'm an eternal optimist, but I'm also a practical realist. I know this book and my suggestions aren't going to work for everyone. Every relationship is unique and has its own set of challenges. It's the same with divorce. No two are exactly alike. For the lucky ones, it can be an easy process, where everything is agreeable and conflict is settled quickly, with both parties walking away fairly unphased and content. For the not-so-lucky ones, a knock-down, drag-out battle that airs every stinky piece of dirty laundry can bring both parties to their knees for years. I've spoken with enough divorced men and women to know that even though mine wasn't one of the best, it also wasn't one of the worst. That's probably why I was eventually able to regroup, put the past behind me, and desire to have a good relationship with my ex.

But what if your situation isn't so rosy? If there was a high level of conflict, cheating, or even abuse, can you still put the dual family principles into play? Can a person work through the pain and

155

anger to have a working relationship with their ex, the person who caused much of that pain? It can be done. Other people have done it, and they and their kids have benefited from it. The real question is, do you want to, and more important, will you? You're the only person who can answer that.

You may be reading this book, thinking that all these principles are great, but you have little or no desire to get along with your ex or vice versa. You may have been hurt too deeply to be able to even think of yourself and your ex being cooperative and friendly, let alone actually liking him or her again. Like I said, I know this isn't going to work for everyone, and you might be one of those who's not going to want to make your family dynamic work this way. That's OK. I'd love to see you give it a try, but the dual family police aren't going to come hunt you down if you don't. However, you can still put the dual family principles to work for you and your kids. After all, a huge benefit of working through the steps and principles is allowing yourself to heal, put the past behind you, and move on to a much happier you and a successful, fulfilling life for you and your kids.

The same principles apply if you want the dual family dynamic to work but your ex is having a tougher time. Remember, you can only control what you do. If you've tried to get along but it just doesn't seem to be working, think about why that may be. Brainstorm about what issues or behaviors derail your communication or interaction with each other. Are there certain events that seem to ignite the spark of discontent? There may be some hidden issues you can uncover if you look hard enough. Do so with an open heart and mind, which I know can be hard to do at times, but try.

Start by making a list of the issues, events, interactions, and even people that seem to get you and your ex off track. If you can discuss these things with your ex, do so in an open and non-threatening way. For instance, you've noticed that everything seems to be fine in your relationship with your ex until the Saturday Little League game each week when he always seems to be stand-offish and annoyed. Bring this up in a caring way by saying something like "I can't help but notice that at the Saturday games you seem a little annoyed, and we don't get along as well as we do the rest of the week. Is there something I'm doing to upset you?"

"Well, I'm Billy's dad, and I think it's my job to take him to practice early and warm up with him and talk to him about the game afterward, but you always have him on Saturdays, and I'm just waiting around for you guys to show up when all the other dads are here with their sons. I'm his dad. I should be doing that with him!"

"Wow, I really had no idea you felt like that. You're right. You should be doing that, and I didn't even realize you were missing out on it. I know Billy would love that extra time with you. How about when I have him on a Saturday, you come and pick him up an hour before the game, take him to the field, then bring him back an hour or so after the game so you guys can play more and have lunch or do whatever? I'll just meet you two there. That will actually give me some time to do some of my own things, too. Will that work better for you?"

"Ya, that would be great. Thanks!"

It may be as simple as that to solve a problem. Asking questions and talking through it is a good start to repairing damage and getting closer as a dual family. With time and doing your best to work through some of your ex's issues, hopefully the bonds of happiness will start to grow. It may never be great or ideal, but if we're always looking at situations with compassion and cooperation, and we're giving to the other person, it's likely to help.

A similar approach is taken when you want the happy dual family dynamic to work, but your ex wants no part of it. This case is a little more extreme than the situation described above, where the ex is just being difficult or having a tough time adjusting to the dual family concept. This type of ex tries to sabotage and manipulate and has little or no regard for how their nasty behavior affects you or your children. This is emotional and difficult, but you can make it a little easier if you set your expectations accordingly. Know that it's very unlikely you're going to get the cooperation you desire from your ex. This way, you're less likely to be let down. Don't ask for much, don't expect much, and learn to accept it. I know how hard this can be. We tend to take on a lot of burden in this type of situation by blaming ourselves for the negative behavior of another, worrying about the kids and how it's affecting them, thinking there's something you're doing wrong, and wishing constantly that things were different. One thing I've learned is that there are unhappy people in this world and there's nothing you can do to change them. As much as you'd like to, as many times as you've tried to be nice and helpful and caring, it doesn't seem to make a difference. They are who they are, and you just have to learn to live with it.

If you are unfortunate enough to be dealing with an ex who wants no part of a happy dual family with you, then all you can do is to create that happy and loving family on your own when your kids are with you. Going through the three-part process, focusing on the vision for your family, knowing the obstacles that are most likely to get in your way, and applying the secrets to your daily life will help you deal with a nasty ex. You'll gain confidence as you test out your new abilities, and you'll be living your new life in a better and healthier way, even if it is one sided.

You'll also want to build up your network of positive people. Having very positive energy around you from people who truly love and care for you will help see you through your challenges. It also may be cathartic to speak with others who are in the same situation. Sometimes it just helps to talk with someone else who knows what you're going through and to feel understood. You can find a variety of groups at Meetup.com, a website dedicated to helping people with like interests meet up locally. Just be sure to keep it positive, and don't get into an ex-bashing frenzy. This should be about support and positivity. You may even want to read some motivational books or listen to CDs or videos that are uplifting. Listening to positive messages rather than the depressing news is a good option to help keep your spirits up, and you might learn some good tips to help you along the way.

I drive a lot for work, and I like to listen to books while I'm on my long trips. I subscribe to a service called Audible (www.Audible.com), where for about $15 a month you can download one book to your computer, iPod, iPad, or other digital device. You can also buy books for sometimes less than that. I love it! When I'm feeling down, insecure, or just need a boost, I look for a book that can lift me up and motivate me. With the push of a button, I have a little extra help to keep me focused in my positive direction. You'll find titles from a range of authors, everyone from bestselling authors like Deepak Chopra and Dale Carnegie—two of my favorites, by the way—to lesser-known books.

The point of all this is when you're dealing with an ex who isn't as rational, loving, and accepting as you are, there may be nothing you can do to make that side of it better. All you can do is focus on making you better and happier, and the same for your kids when they're with you. The sooner you can accept that and not try to change and fight it, the better off you'll be.

Even in the most extreme relationships, you can come out on top. It is your resolve, your strength and vision that will help pull you through in the most difficult times you can imagine, as you'll see in the next chapter with my good friend Jessica. This story is heartbreaking, horrifying, and true. She is truly inspiring. I've learned a lot from her, and I hope you will, too.

Dual Family
Steps to Success

▸ When dealing with a difficult ex, remember, you can only control what you do.

▸ Think about the times that seem to cause the most trouble or tension for you and your ex. Write them down and ask your ex for suggestions to resolve the conflict.

▸ Set your expectations appropriately, and don't expect too much from a nasty ex who wants no part of creating a dual family.

▸ Surround yourself with positive people and messages that will lift your spirits.

CHAPTER 17

Jessica's Story

"Life is not the way it's supposed to be. It's the way it is.
The way you deal with it is what makes the difference."
—VIRGINIA SATIR

Jessica met the man of her dreams right out of college. Joseph was a handsome, athletic man from Brazil. They met in college, and over the course of a couple of years, became close friends and started dating. She described him as picture perfect. He was captivating and charming and swept her off her feet. He took her on romantic dates every week to her favorite places, and they went camping and hiking together, and they even shared a passion for their church. She got along great with his friends, and he got along great with hers. Over the years their friendship grew, their love affair intensified, and they were both incredibly happy and in love. It was the romance she had always dreamed of.

Jessica thought she did all the right things. She took years to get to know him and grow a friendship before they started dating, and she made sure they had built a strong foundation of respect, love, and trust before they married. She came from a divorced family, and although her experience as a child of divorce was a good one, it was important to her that her marriage didn't suffer the same fate. She felt strongly that if she built a good relationship based on friendship, respect, and love with a man, she would never get divorced. She felt very secure that marrying him was the right thing to do.

Their courtship was romantic and full of fun and excitement, but Jessica said that the relationship started to change almost immediately after they were married. She recalls that within minutes of saying "I do," things soured. He was different. After the ceremony she embraced him, but he was cold and disconnected from her. She brushed it off and thought maybe he was just overwhelmed by everything, but the disconnectedness grew. Week by week, month by month the passionate, fun relationship they had before they were married started to disappear. They weren't communicating like they had before they were married. They rarely did anything fun as a couple, and the day-to-day affection was disappearing as well. According to Jessica, Joseph also became very controlling, especially with their finances. Even though Jessica was making most of the money at the time, she had no idea how much was in the bank. He wouldn't even let her look at the checkbook. By this point, she was very unhappy and didn't know what to do. She was miserable but didn't want to consider divorce. As many of us do, she felt she could fix things if she just gave it enough time.

Many couples believe that a baby will bring them closer together and hope that children will be the glue to fix a broken marriage. Jessica and Joseph were no different. She had always dreamed of being a mom and saw having children as an opportunity to bring her and her husband closer together and fulfill her dream as well. She thought since she and Joe had both desperately wanted children, it could only improve things. Their first baby, Eva, came about a year and a half into the marriage. Their relationship didn't improve, but it didn't get worse, either. They shared moments of closeness and normalcy, but after their second baby, Ethan, things changed. The intensity of parenthood and the pressures of a new family only made things worse. Jessica said Joseph became verbally abusive, more controlling, and was away from the house more and more. Jessica felt like a single parent most of the time. Joe had a new job and threw himself into every party and event associated with it. He started coming home late at night and was rarely around to help Jessica with their family. She was stressed, physically and emotionally, and it was taking its toll on her. She began to physically change. She started to look weak, disheveled, and beaten down. She was becoming defeated. This once polished, confident woman was losing herself not to her children but to the husband and marriage she was trying to save.

She clung to hope that the marriage could be saved, but when the abuse turned physical, she knew she had to do something. She said he started to push her, sometimes so hard, she was forced to the ground, her knees bloodied by the impact. She was mentally, emotionally, and now physically abused. She was praying daily for a sign, some kind of guidance or help. She knew she was going to have to do something, but she didn't know what. She was fearful for her own safety and that of her children. What had happened to the beautiful life she and her perfect husband had planned together? This wasn't a dream life. She was living a nightmare! She was thrilled to have her two children, but they weren't a family. Joseph was rarely around, and when he was home, he didn't participate in activities with her and the kids, and he didn't take on the role of husband or father. She was coming to the realization that her hopes and dreams for the life she had always planned were gone. She was devastated.

Jessica had one last glimmer of hope when Joseph took her to an attorney to plan their estate together. She thought maybe he was turning over a new leaf, planning for their future together. The appointment went well, and they created a plan for retirement and saving for the kids' college education. She was finally hopeful that things would change for the better. A couple of weeks later a package from the estate planner came in the mail. As she was leafing through the mail on the counter, she touched the envelope from the attorney and felt a shock run up her arm like she had touched a live wire. She had an eerie feeling. She got such a negative, gut sense from the envelope that she didn't want to touch it again. Later that night, Joseph asked her to sign what was in the envelope. She refused. He exploded! He yelled and screamed at her to sign it. She adamantly refused, sharply reminded of the terrible feeling she got earlier from the package. He flew into a rage and demanded she sign it. She was terrified by his anger. She knew she needed to get out of the marriage but didn't know how. Joseph controlled everything. She was at home with two children and not working. She didn't have a lot of options, and she felt trapped.

One evening, Joseph was still away from home with their oldest child, Eva. It was 6 pm, and Jessica had expected them back hours earlier and had been calling Joseph to find out where they were but couldn't reach him. She was playing with Ethan in the family room when she saw her husband walk up the driveway, but Eva was not with him. She instantly got a feeling somewhere between nervousness and dread. She opened the front door to find out what was happening. "What's going on? Where's Eva?" she asked her husband. Joseph said nothing as he quickly walked around the house and grabbed things, seemingly at random. "What's going on? What are you doing? Where's Eva? Joseph, talk to me!" Jessica said frantically, not knowing what was happening or about to happen. Joseph walked around the house for just a couple of minutes without saying anything to Jessica until he grabbed Ethan and told Jessica he was leaving her. As he walked out the door with Ethan in his arms, he threw some papers on the floor. As the door slammed, she stood in the hallway, stunned and in shock, frozen, unable to even respond. She bent down to pick up the papers he had thrown on the floor and was horrified when she read them. It was a restraining order to keep her away from her children for a month. She would only be allowed a supervised, two-hour visit a few times a week.

Apparently Joe had convinced a judge that Jessica was mentally unstable and at risk of harming the kids and potentially kidnapping them. He was hoping that a restraining order would push her over the edge and cause her to do something foolish, proving he was right. Then he would have valid grounds to file for full custody of the kids. She couldn't believe her eyes. "What the hell is going on?" she asked out loud in a now-empty house. She still couldn't believe what had just happened.

Jessica was in a daze as she tried to process the last few minutes.

Her head was spinning as she realized that her husband was divorcing her, her two children had just been taken from her, and she had a restraining order that prevented her from seeing her children. Her life as she knew it was gone. She slumped down on the floor and began to sob. She could barely breathe. She kept thinking, "He has my kids! I can't see my kids! Where are my kids?" As a mother, this was the worst kind of torture she could experience. She had only been away from them for a few hours at a time since they had been born. How was she going to live without them for four weeks? How were they going to live without her? She felt paralyzed. Joseph left without telling her where he was taking the kids, so she wasn't even sure she would ever see them again.

She started to panic as reality set in. She read the restraining order again. She realized this wasn't a nightmare. She wasn't going to wake up from a dream. This was real! Her uncertainty turned to fear, fear turned to panic, and now her panic turned to rage. She felt a deep well of anger, and hatred begin to swell inside her. She paced around, looking for something to give her guidance, a next step. She yelled throughout the empty house, "You can't take my kids! I'll show you! You can't take my kids!"

She recalled the last few years of her marriage and how distant Joseph had been, how she didn't feel connected to him, how he was rarely home and paid little attention to her and their children. She remembered the emotional abuse, the verbal lashings, and the physical abuse she had endured all while trying to keep her marriage and family together. The love she once felt for her perfect relationship and husband quickly turned to anger. She just couldn't believe her kids were gone. She had no idea where they were, and even if she did, she wouldn't be able to see them. She cried so hard, she could barely breathe. Exhausted, drained, and spent, she fell asleep on the floor.

The next morning brought only enough clarity for her to know she needed help—and fast. She needed an attorney, but Joseph had taken all the checks, credit cards, cash, and even the coins in her purse. She was literally penniless. A good friend loaned her some money until she got back on her feet. She hired an attorney, and they got to work on getting the kids back. The judge presiding over the case could tell that Jessica wasn't unstable, but she said that Joseph's attorney insisted that a court-appointed supervisor be stationed at her house to review her interactions with the boys to see if they were, in fact, in any kind of danger from her. Could you imagine after going through all this, she was now forced to have a stranger in her home to supervise her time with her children? She really could have gone crazy from all the stress and pressure, but she knew she had to keep her wits about her if she was going to win back her children.

Finally, luck was in her favor when the supervisor witnessed a tirade by Joseph at their house. He was yelling, screaming, and throwing things. As he left the house, he yelled to Jessica, "I'm going to kill you, bitch!" It turns out that Jessica had good reason to fear for her life. Remember that envelope from the estate planner that gave her such an eerie feeling? Inside was a power of attorney giving Joseph complete control over everything and a life insurance policy against Jessica for $1 million! She knows she is incredibly fortunate to be alive today.

The court-appointed supervisor testified in Jessica's favor, and she won back shared custody of her children, but she says the verbal and mental abuse from Joseph continues. He's called child protective services to say she's abusing the children. He's called the police to say she was driving drunk. Every time he does this she has to fight the charges and incur the expenses to go back to court if necessary. It hasn't been easy, but she's made it work.

Through all this and years of abuse and torment, Jessica has persevered by focusing on what she could control and change— her life! She eventually went back to school to get her degree to become a CPA, and she now owns her own firm. She is incredibly successful and happy in her career. She recently went back to the hobbies that she loved so much as a child, which bring her a lot of happiness and joy. Her house is warm and welcoming with pictures of her and the kids everywhere. Her kitchen is a tribute to her strength and intention to live the best life possible. Plaques are scattered on walls and shelves with sayings like: "Soar. One's attitude determines one's altitude."

Although she still wears the physical and mental scars of her abuse, she hasn't let them hold her back from living her best life. I truly admire her for persevering the way she has, putting herself and her children first, pulling herself out of a messy marriage and divorce, and improving her life. She has defined her own happiness and success instead of allowing her life to be defined by her ex-husband and her negative past, which is still very much a part of her present.

Jessica doesn't have a happy dual family with her ex-husband. They don't see eye to eye on anything, but the truly amazing thing is that despite that, she has managed to put the principles in this book to work in her attitude toward her ex and in her relationship with herself and her kids. Even after all he's done to hurt her, she refuses to bad-mouth her ex in front of the children, she has surrounded herself with amazing people who support and encourage her, and she has worked on herself to become a happier and more fulfilled person.

Jessica's experience is proof that even in the worst circumstances you can come back and live a happy and fulfilled life. When you feel all is lost, just know that it isn't. You must pull yourself out of that feeling and surround yourself with people who can help you emerge a stronger, happier version of you. Go back to those positivity partners you created before and find more if you need them. It won't be easy, it may take some time, but Jessica did it after all she's been though, and I bet you can, too.

Dual Family
STEPS TO SUCCESS

▸ When faced with a seemingly impossible situation with your ex, focus on being the best person you can be. Go through the three-part process and make sure you have a strong vision of the family you want to create with your children.

▸ Use the secrets and build your skills to help you deal with your ex.

▸ Stay positive!

CHAPTER 18

Designing the Life of Your Dreams

"Go confidently in the direction of your dreams.
Live the life you have imagined."
—HENRY DAVID THOREAU

This chapter isn't about divorce; it's about life and what you'd like your ideal life to be. Let's face it, going through a divorce, even a fairly amicable one can shake your sense of self for years. It's a huge emotional drain not only for you but for your children, family, and even your friends who are helping you through it. When you're a parent going through a divorce, you're usually taking care of your kids and their emotions first and putting yourself last. But we can't forget about ourselves. You know the saying you have to take care of yourself before you can take care of others? It's kind of like when you're on a plane and the flight attendant instructs you to put on your oxygen mask first before you help your child. This isn't selfish; in fact it's essential! You have to take care of your own needs before you can reach your highest potential and give your best self to your children, family, friends, and the rest of the world. After all, they certainly deserve the best of you, and you absolutely deserve to be the very best that you can be.

If your life isn't going exactly the way you had imagined it—you've sidelined dreams, postponed passions, and been too afraid to go after what you really want—now is a great time to change all that and start making your life more of what you truly want it to be.

I love living big, going for the things I want in life, and driving my passions forward.

I've surrounded myself with people I care for deeply and who touch me in a rich and satisfying way. My life now is incredibly satisfying, and I can honestly say I'm truly happy.

It wasn't always like this, though. I've realized that one of the reasons I left my marriage was because I wasn't happy with much of anything. I didn't see it at the time, but I wasn't happy with my life. It was very plain vanilla, average. There was little excitement, and I seemed to live for tomorrow and things to come, instead of being happy and satisfied in the present. I remember I used to tell myself, I'll be happy when we finally go on that vacation or I get that new job or when we move. I found little pleasure and happiness in day-to-day life, and without having a clear cause of this, I blamed it on my marriage. I thought that leaving my marriage would fix everything and I'd be happy, but that didn't happen. It took me years to realize I had unfulfilled passions and dreams that needed to be pursued, and it wasn't until I started doing things that fed those passions and dreams that I started to feel fulfilled and began to love my life and be happy.

I have to admit I spent an awful lot of my life hoping and wishing for true, sustainable happiness, thinking it was something that happened to me, not something I could control. But year by year as I took more control of my life and fed my passions, I realized I did have power over my happiness, how successful or unsuccessful I was, how much money I had, the type of people in my life, my career, everything! That may seem obvious, but we don't tend to live our lives as though this is true. Think about it. How many times have you stayed too long in a job you hated simply because you knew you were safe there, it was comfortable, or you were too nervous to try something else? What about an unhappy relationship? Did you ever spend too much time with negative friends who always seem to talk down about everyone and everything around them? How did that affect you? Why have you stayed in these relationships and situations? Possibly because you were scared or nervous to make a change, believing that the outcome could be even worse than what you were currently experiencing. Or maybe it was because you didn't think you had control over these things or how you fit into them. But you have control! What you choose to do with your life makes all the difference in the world as to whether you live an average, regular existence, or you live an exciting, successful, and passionate life. I have deliberately chose the latter.

When I tell people that my ex husband and I get along great, they generally say, "Oh, that must be wonderful for your son." That's absolutely true. Evan is happy, healthy, and well-adjusted in large part because our family is the same way. But he's not the only one who's happy. I'm happy! What started out as a desire for my ex and I to get along for the sake of our son turned into changing my whole life. I'm living a life better than I ever imagined possible, and it gets greater every year. Believe it or not, I owe a lot of this to the wonderful relationship I have with my ex and his new wife. Because we don't argue, I have more positive than negative energy in my life. Because I'm not worried or stressed about my relationship with my ex, how my child is dealing with our dual family, or other issues many divorced families face, I'm able to take all that positive energy and focus it to create the best life I possibly can for my family, my son, and myself.

I met a woman recently who had been divorced for a couple of years. We hit it off and started talking about our families. I was telling her about all the fun I was having, the great people I was meeting, and how happy Evan and I were. She was amazed at everything I told her I was doing. "How did you get your life back together?" she asked. "You're so happy. I want that!"

I replied, "It took some time. I worked on it for years, and I continue to work on it and look for different ways to grow and pursue my passions and find like-minded people to do great things with."

She responded, "How do you meet these people and find the time to do all these things?" I could tell she was truly interested and might be ready for a change. She wanted to start dating and meet someone special, and she wanted to start having fun again. But she just didn't have time to do all that. "I was with my kids every night this summer! How am I supposed to meet new people and do new things if I have my kids all the time?" she asked.

I paused and asked her candidly, "Did you need to have your kids every night for two months straight?"

"What do you mean?" she responded.

"When I'm upset or feeling a little unsure, I want to be with my son more," I said. "I want his company and the comfort that being with him brings me. It's a lot easier than forcing myself to do something new that might be a little scary, even if I know it would be good for me or really fun. He's my comfort zone, which is great but not if I allow myself to stay in that zone and don't push myself to grow and change. You know what I mean?" She looked at me questioningly. I could tell she was thinking about what I had just said. So I asked her again, "Did you really need to be with your kids every night, or was that an easy choice?"

She smiled with recognition. "I get it," she said. "I need to make some changes." Think about your circumstances. Are you making the easy, safe, and comfortable choices in life, or are you designing and creating the best possible life you can?

Close your eyes for a minute, clear your thoughts, and ask yourself, Is your life right now everything you want it to be? If you're reading this book, then you're probably going through a tough time and life isn't perfect. That's why this is a great time to ask that question. This is a time to point yourself in a new direction and start creating more of the things you really want out of life.

It might be a little hard to envision that new life now. You're divorced, dealing with your emotions your kids' emotions, and putting the pieces back together again. You may not be ready to make some hard-core plans yet, and that's fine. Just do some daydreaming right now if things seem impossible and out of reach, but just know that your dreams and goals may be much easier to reach than you realize. Maybe you're a fantastic cook, and you've always wanted to have your own cooking show. It's not hard with all the technology available today. You could start it on YouTube. Maybe you love to read, and you've always wanted to start a book club. Start a club on Meetup.com or at your local bookstore. Wanted to run a marathon since you were 12? Join a local running club. Whatever your goals and dreams are or have been, you can start living them, and there's no time better than now.

Don't stop there: In your happiest and most fulfilling life, what are you doing? What kind of job do you have? Where are you living? What kinds of friends do you have, and what's your relationship with them like? What's your relationship with your children like? How is your financial situation? What are your passions, and how are you fulfilling them? Are you in a romantic relationship? I know this might seem a little odd to be asking yourself these questions, but you can't create something if you don't even think about it first, right?

Remember the quote from Jim Rohn, "Happiness is something you design." You have to think about what you want before you can start designing it and put it into action. So let's do it. Take out your journal right now and start writing down things you'd like to do in life, your list of goals and dreams. Don't bother with how these things will happen; just think, dream, and write them down. Remember the vision you created for your happy dual family? This is your vision for you! This is how you want your life to be. Don't hold back. Have fun with it! Write down everything you can think of that you want to do or accomplish before you leave this earth. It's likely going to be a long list, so start it now and keep it handy so you can add to it from time to time when you think of new things.

If all this seems a little overwhelming, just relax and think about planning your life, goals, and dreams as you would a vacation. I spoke with a client of mine the other day, and she was telling me how excited she was to go on vacation in two more weeks. She could hardly wait. She and her husband had been planning this trip to Maui for months. They searched and searched for the perfect resort, they had smartly saved up all their mileage points so they could fly first class, they looked at reviews for sightseeing trips and excursions, and they were even considering taking scuba diving lessons. This being their first trip to Maui, they got recommendations from friends on where to eat and shop, they rented a fun Jeep to drive around the island in, and they were ready to go. In fact, the night before we spoke, she said she had printed out the plane tickets to show her husband. They took months planning every last detail of their one-week trip to paradise.

Does that sound familiar? If you'd spend this much time planning a vacation, how much time will you put into planning your life? I certainly don't expect you to spend months planning the next 40 years of your life, but you can spend some time now and maybe a little time each week thinking about, planning, and working toward your goals and dreams so you can create the great life you want to live. You don't get a chance to do this over. Every day lasts only 24 hours, and you can't ever get them back! Don't let your days, weeks, months, years, and eventually decades pass by without you realizing your full potential, living your passions, and achieving your goals.

This is where it gets really exciting! You're going to create a plan for you to live your best life. Are you ready? I hope so because your life will never be the same once you do this and follow through. Creating a plan for your life can seem like an overwhelming task at first, but I'm going to help you break it down so you can easily create it, and just as important, execute it.

Before we begin, I want to give special thanks to my mentor, Brian Buffini. Brian is a business coach, primarily in the real estate world, but he's also a life coach. He taught me how to write goals, and much of what I've listed here in the book for you to do, I learned from him. I adapted his suggestions to create a model that works best for me. You can do the same—adjust my suggestions to create a plan that works best for you. The point is to commit to living a life that is focused on achieving goals and creating your best life.

Let's start with something easy and just brainstorm for a few minutes. Close your eyes, relax, and think about you in your ideal life. What does that look like? What city are you living in? Where are you working? What kind of a home do you live in? Just dream and think about all the wonderful, amazing things you would be doing in your dream life. There are no limits here, remember. Don't think about how you'll make these things happen, and don't stop yourself by saying, I could never do that. Just dream and have fun. Have you ever wanted to own your own company? Don't think about how that might happen; just think about wanting to own a company. Would you like to have an amazing, romantic relationship? Don't think about how you'd actually meet that person; just think about that perfect relationship and how great that would feel. Getting the idea? Also add the things you'd like to do on a regular basis but maybe you haven't put enough focus on, like exercising three times a week. Write down anything you want to accomplish and do in your life, all the things that will help you to feel happy and fulfilled.

When you're ready, and you think you've spent a good amount of time dreaming, maybe 10 to 20 minutes, start writing it all down. You can find a list of some ideas in the "Goals and Dreams Worksheet" on the Resources page at www.DualFamily.com/book-resources, or you can write them in your journal, but you'll want to keep them somewhere you can easily access the list. You don't need to prioritize them. Just write down many as you can. For some people, this may seem a little forced, and you may feel pressure to write down everything. If you do, just take a deep breath and relax. Yes, this is big stuff we're doing here, but it doesn't all have to happen today. In fact, your goal and dream list is likely to evolve, which is why you want to keep the list handy. Add to this list whenever you think of new ideas for things you'd like to do, accomplish, or have in your life, and if you change your mind about something, just scratch it off.

When you have a decent size list together, say 30 or more items, I want you to begin to think of them in categories. You'll classify each item into one of seven categories: health, business, financial, relationships, fun, personal growth, and spiritual. Check out the following list for examples of activities that go into each category:

1. *Health:* Lose 20 pounds, exercise three times a week, quit smoking
2. *Business:* Get a $3,000 raise, get a promotion, start my own business
3. *Financial:* Pay off my debt, save 10 percent in my 401(k), buy a home
4. *Relationships:* Cook dinner as a family each night, reconnect with self, build my happy dual family
5. *Fun:* Go on a family vacation, visit with friends at least once a month, throw a party
6. *Personal growth:* Learn French, run a marathon, read one book a month
7. *Spiritual:* Go to church each week, support a local charity, learn to meditate

If you'd like to add an "other" category or something different, feel free to change one or more of them. This is a plan for you, so you can customize it any way you like.

Now, start putting each item on your list into one of these categories. It's OK if you have a longer list in some categories and a shorter one in others. We're not going for balance here. Actually, an unbalanced list can be telling. If you've got a very long list in a particular category, it may mean that's an area in which you feel you have a lot of work to do. For instance, if you've got twenty items written under financial and only five to ten in the other categories, it may mean you've been lacking in that area, and that's where you may want to focus a little more. Conversely, if you have only two or three items in a particular category, you may feel you're doing quite well in that area.

Once you have all your dreams and goals listed under one of the seven categories, look at the whole list. Reflect for a moment on the area where you have the most items listed vs. the least, and think about the areas you'd like to focus on the most. Now, we're going to go category by category and think about which are the most important items in that list. Start with health. If you have eight items listed under health, which of those are the most important for you to work on? Choose two, maybe three items, and put a little star next to them so you remember what they are. Do this for all the categories until you have at least a couple items in each category.

This next step involves knowing a little bit about yourself and how you tend to deal with tackling new tasks. Everyone handles this in a different way. Some people can't take on too much, or they get overloaded and frustrated, and they just give up, while others are consummate overachievers who will take on as much as they possibly can. You may also fall somewhere in between. Which are you?

You're about to choose the goals and dreams you want to start working on first, so it's best to match the difficulty of the activity with your task-tolerance level. The goal isn't to get everything on your list completed as fast as possible. The idea here is that you're consistently working to grow, improving yourself and your life, and working toward creating your dreams so you can live your best possible life every day. Honestly, I find consistency to be the hardest part. So if you've got a ton going on in your life, and you know you can't take on much more or you'll crack, you may want to start with something smaller or easier. However, if you're an overachiever and you're ready to tackle something big, go for it! Of the two to three items you identified as most important in each category, choose one of those items in each category to start working on first, and write them all down separately.

You'll find a step-by-step guide in the "Goal Planning Worksheet" on the Resources page at www.DualFamily.com/book-resources.

Once you have these seven items you're going to tackle first, think about when you'd like to have that goal accomplished and checked off your list. Is it something small, like subscribe to and read *Success* magazine each month? (This is one of my favorite magazines, by the way, and I recommend it highly.) You can easily subscribe online (www.Success.com), or run down to your local bookstore, grab the latest copy, and mail in the subscription card. Boom, done! Or you may want to start with something that's going to take a little more planning and effort, like lose 30 pounds. With something like this, you'll want to write down a plan to get there, with the steps needed to accomplish that goal. To do this, first set a due date, say one year from today. What do you need to do today to start working on that goal? You'll probably want to speak with your doctor, so making an appointment to see your physician would be a good first step. You may also want to research various weight-loss plans, speak with friends who've been successful with weight loss, and review all your options. Put a time limit on this so it doesn't drag on forever. Let's give the research period a one-week completion goal. Then you need to decide on a course of action to lose 30 pounds in one year. That's only 2.5 pounds a month. When you break it down, it's tiny, isn't it? That's what we're doing here. We're breaking the goals down into manageable pieces so you can more easily tackle each one and start living a life of accomplishment.

Write down a step-by-step course of action for each item. This may take a little while, especially if you've decided to go after some lofty goals and dreams. If you begin to feel overwhelmed, just dial it back and start with one or two items instead of seven. Remember, there's no pressure here. I'd much rather you start with something small, get it done straight away, and feel that great sense of accomplishment when you check it off the list, rather than get frustrated because there's so much to do, you don't know where to start.

Now that you've done all the background work, you're going to set it into daily, weekly, monthly, and yearly accomplishment sheets. I know, this is in-depth and maybe even a little intense, but remember the example of planning a vacation. If you can take months to plan a vacation, you can take a couple of days to do this. You can create your own daily, weekly, monthly, and yearly accomplishments sheets, or you can download them from the Resources page at www.DualFamily.com/book-resources.

Let's start with the yearly sheet. In one year from today's date, write down any items that will take approximately that long to accomplish. For the sake of simplicity, let's use the goal of saving $3,000 in one year. On your monthly accomplishment sheet, you'll write down what you need to do to reach that goal each month. Three thousand breaks down to $250 each month. Write down "save $250/month" on your monthly sheet. What will it take each week to hit that goal? It comes out to around $60 a week, so write down "save $60/week" on your weekly goal sheet. Starting to look a little more doable, isn't it? OK, you know what's coming next. On the daily accomplishment sheet write down what you can do each day to help you reach that yearly goal. It's about $8 a day. Think about how you can save $8 a day and, you guessed, make a list. Maybe it's making your own lunch at home instead of going out, or it can be a combination of activities, like only buying things that are on sale at the grocery store and using coupons or canceling your cable service (yikes!). When you break down a goal into manageable pieces, you're much more likely to do what it takes to help you reach your goal. It takes a little time and practice, but with consistency and focus, in no time at all you'll be checking items off your lists and working toward some great goals and dreams. So dream big and go for it!

All this planning has another great effect you might not be aware of. In a very uncertain time in your life, this gives you a sense of control. You're the one in the driver's seat now, and you're on your way to making big decisions and changes in your life. It's empowering and fulfilling! Your focus is on you and designing this amazing life instead of on your ex. Isn't that reason enough to do all this? Absolutely! Every day you'll be doing things that enrich you and your life and make you happy and fulfilled. This is the best gift you could possibly give yourself. As you grow, accomplish, and develop, you'll not only be enriching your own life, but you'll also be enriching your children and everyone else around you. Living your best life isn't about looking to the future; it's about creating happiness for you right now and creating ways to grow that happiness in the future.

I know this is a lot of work, but it's worth it, I promise you. I've outlined the way I like to write my goals, but you can do it any way you choose. In this very digital world we live in, I'm still very much a paper girl. I have a binder of all my goals and dreams and game plans for how to accomplish them. I look at my daily and weekly goals regularly and check in on my monthly and yearly goals every couple of weeks to make sure I'm on track. Once you have them written down and organized, it's just a matter of to-dos and keeping the daily and weekly tasks front of mind. I like to keep my worksheets on my bed stand. They're the last thing I see at night and the first thing I see in the morning. I have friends who like to put their goals on their bathroom mirrors so they are forced to look at them every day. You do what feels comfortable to you as long as you are able to look at them daily. Keeping these items front of mind and doing the tasks necessary for you to achieve the goal is essential.

This is a good time for a word of warning. Goal and dream planning can be intimidating, and knowing that we're doing things that will change our lives, even if we know it's for the better, can sometimes scare us away from taking the action necessary to move forward. It's easy to talk yourself out of a goal and say, I'll do that tomorrow and brush off a task or even become nervous at the thought of reaching a big goal. That was the case for me in writing this book. There were many points where it all seemed so overwhelming and daunting that I talked myself into not finishing it just to avoid any possible negative outcomes. I got nervous and thought, What if no one likes the book? What If I open myself up to the world and no one cares? I started to scare myself out of finishing. But this was a goal for me, and I truly believe my story can help other divorced families, so I had to buck up, keep writing—and here we are!

We hold ourselves back a lot in life, whether it be from fear, lack of knowledge, resources, or something else. Don't do that now. You have a fresh start in life. This is your time to shine! Make the most out of this experience, just as you would make the most out of that fantastic vacation you so diligently planned. It's the best feeling in the world to have your life come together just the way you want it. Life is never perfect, but you can make it pretty darn great.

While you're working on your tasks to accomplish your goals and dreams, try to recognize where you hold yourself back. What are you nervous or scared about? When I know I'm holding myself back from something, I often ask myself, What's the worst thing that can happen if I do this? It's usually not much when I think about it. Coming to terms with your own fears and weaknesses isn't fun to do, but it's absolutely essential if you're going to successfully design and execute your best life.

You'll never be able to live your very best life if you don't work through your fears and allow them to hold you back. I'm determined to not allow my fears to hold me back. I want to look back on my life without regrets and know that I made the most I possibly could out of this one life, this one chance I had to be on this earth. You can, too. We just have to put our fears aside, design that great life, and make it happen. I'm willing to do that. Are you?

It all starts with designing your happy dual family and building from there. It's going to take some time and be uncomfortable and scary, but I know you'll be better for it just as I have been. Join me in creating a movement of happy dual families and people who are creating and living their best life possible! We only get one chance, so let's make it count!

Dual Family
STEPS TO SUCCESS

- ▸ Brainstorm for about 10 to 20 minutes about all the things you'd like to accomplish, do, or have in your life now and in the future, then write them down.

- ▸ Classify each into one of the seven categories and put a star next to the ones most important to you.

- ▸ Choose one item from each category to work on first.

- ▸ Create a yearly, monthly, weekly, and daily task list for each item.

- ▸ Review your lists daily to ensure they are front of mind, and be consistent in working on them.

- ▸ Live a life you love!

Join *The Dual Family* community and connect with other divorced individuals and families who are creating happiness after divorce.

Website	www.DualFamily.com
Facebook	Facebook.com/DualFamily
Twitter	DualFamily
YouTube	DD Richards

I look forward to connecting with you!

DD Richards

Join me in my mission to turn divorced families into happy dual families. Give the following pages to friends, family, co-workers or acquaintances who may benefit from *The Dual Family Guide*. Let's build happier, healthier divorced families—one family at a time.

DD Richards

*Divorced dad Rob N. says, "**The Dual Family Guide**
is a must read for divorcees."*

Put the drama and struggle of divorce behind you! You *can* create a happy family and a happier you after divorce. A new book, *The Dual Family Guide to Creating a Happy Family After Divorce Under Two Roofs,* will show you how.

In the book, you'll learn to:
- Emotionally work through your divorce.
- Avoid the drama that often plagues divorced families.
- Overcome common obstacles in your family.
- Create a fantastic life for yourself!

You'll also gain skills in scheduling, conflict resolution, and communication with your ex. Each chapter has a set of action items to help you through the challenges.

For more information about the book, go to www. DualFamily.com, where you'll also find videos and helpful information about creating happiness in divorced families.

Buy the book on Amazon.com, or ask for it in your local bookstore.

Connect with other divorced individuals and families who are creating happiness after divorce:

Website	www.DualFamily.com
Facebook	Facebook.com/DualFamily
Twitter	DualFamily
YouTube	DD Richards

*Divorced dad Rob N. says, "***The Dual Family Guide***
is a must read for divorcees."

Put the drama and struggle of divorce behind you! You *can* create a happy family and a happier you after divorce. A new book, *The Dual Family Guide to Creating a Happy Family After Divorce Under Two Roofs,* will show you how.

In the book, you'll learn to:
- Emotionally work through your divorce.
- Avoid the drama that often plagues divorced families.
- Overcome common obstacles in your family.
- Create a fantastic life for yourself!

You'll also gain skills in scheduling, conflict resolution, and communication with your ex. Each chapter has a set of action items to help you through the challenges.

For more information about the book, go to www. DualFamily.com, where you'll also find videos and helpful information about creating happiness in divorced families.

Buy the book on Amazon.com, or ask for it in your local bookstore.

Connect with other divorced individuals and families who are creating happiness after divorce:

Website	www.DualFamily.com
Facebook	Facebook.com/DualFamily
Twitter	DualFamily
YouTube	DD Richards

*Divorced dad Rob N. says, "**The Dual Family Guide**
is a must read for divorcees."*

Put the drama and struggle of divorce behind you! You *can* create a happy family and a happier you after divorce. A new book, *The Dual Family Guide to Creating a Happy Family After Divorce Under Two Roofs,* will show you how.

In the book, you'll learn to:
- Emotionally work through your divorce.
- Avoid the drama that often plagues divorced families.
- Overcome common obstacles in your family.
- Create a fantastic life for yourself!

You'll also gain skills in scheduling, conflict resolution, and communication with your ex. Each chapter has a set of action items to help you through the challenges.

For more information about the book, go to www. DualFamily.com, where you'll also find videos and helpful information about creating happiness in divorced families.

Buy the book on Amazon.com, or ask for it in your local bookstore.

Connect with other divorced individuals and families who are creating happiness after divorce:

Website	www.DualFamily.com
Facebook	Facebook.com/DualFamily
Twitter	DualFamily
YouTube	DD Richards

Made in the USA
San Bernardino, CA
21 July 2013